IMAGES
of America

JOSHUA TREE NATIONAL PARK

Two desert ecosystems, the high-elevation Mojave Desert and the low-lying Colorado Desert, meet at Joshua Tree National Park. The jumbled monzogranite boulders and twisted forms of the Joshua tree form the backdrop for the western half of the park, its Mojave Desert section. This area has been called the Wonderland of Rocks. Found here are mazelike canyons and valleys where new discoveries await at every turn. (Photograph by Phil Dunham, courtesy of the National Park Service.)

ON THE COVER: On October 31, 1936, a desert traveler contemplates a Joshua tree in the Queen Valley area of Joshua Tree National Monument. (Photograph by George Grant, courtesy of the National Park Service.)

IMAGES
of America

JOSHUA TREE
NATIONAL PARK

Joseph W. Zarki

ARCADIA
PUBLISHING

Copyright © 2015 by Joseph W. Zarki
ISBN 978-1-4671-3281-7

Published by Arcadia Publishing
Charleston, South Carolina

Printed in the United States of America

Library of Congress Control Number: 2014954333

For all general information, please contact Arcadia Publishing:
Telephone 843-853-2070
Fax 843-853-0044
E-mail sales@arcadiapublishing.com
For customer service and orders:
Toll-Free 1-888-313-2665

Visit us on the Internet at www.arcadiapublishing.com

*This book is dedicated to the employees, volunteers, and partners
of Joshua Tree National Park and Monument, past and present.
Like the Joshua tree itself, you symbolize this great park.*

CONTENTS

ACKNOWLEDGMENTS

Most of the pictures and many references consulted in this book came from National Park Service collections at Joshua Tree and at the National Park Service Historic Photograph Collection in Harpers Ferry, West Virginia. Unless otherwise noted, all images are courtesy of the National Park Service (NPS). At Harpers Ferry, Wade Myers spent several days working with me in July 2013, and Tom Patterson provided map data for Joshua Tree. Other National Park Service support came from Colleen Hyde at the Grand Canyon and Lee Whittlesey at Yellowstone.

Former colleagues at Joshua Tree National Park who lent a hand include Jennifer Albrinck, Cathy Bell, Andrea Compton, George Land, Karin Messaros, Paul Morley, Lorna Shuman, and Pam Tripp. Special thanks go to the park's curator, Melanie Spoo, who gave countless hours of her time over the last two years. Mel went out of her way to find sources or direct me to information she thought would be helpful. For this, I am most grateful. Meg Foley and Marian Tremblay at the Joshua Tree National Park Association provided records and photographs.

The Twentynine Palms Historical Society contributed many photographs and made room for me whenever I camped at their library. Les Snodgrass, Pat Rimmington, and Marilyn Collier were always helpful and infallibly cheerful. Laurie Geeson and the volunteers at the Morongo Basin Historical Society allowed me full access to their collection and even provided lunch.

Other institutions lending photographs and archival help include the Van Lahr Collection; the Digital Collections, Library of Congress; the Smithsonian Institution, Historical Collection; Christine Giles, Katherine Hough, and Shelley Orlowski at the Palm Springs Art Museum; Eric Milenkiewicz of Special Collections & Archives, University of California, Riverside; LeeAnn Clarke at Action 29 Palms, Mike Pierson and Jacque Schindewolf at the General Patton Museum, Cara Stansberry at the Agua Caliente Cultural Museum, Steve Williamson at the Temecula Valley Museum, Chris Clarke and Zach Behrens at KCET, Terry Frewin and Joan Taylor of the Sierra Club, the Sharlot Hall Museum and Library, the Santa Clarita Historical Society, Larissa Glasser at the Arnold Arboretum Horticultural Library, and Sofia Yalouris of the Maine Historical Society.

Photograph assistance came from the following people: Dana Bowden, Dave Brolan, Frances Carmichael, Bob and Maureen Cates, Donna and Larry Charpied, Robb Hannawacker, Patty Hughes, Judy Jamison, Ralph Kagan, Art Kidwell, Luka at U2360Gradi, Jeff McLane, Candice and Rod Smith, Paul Smith, and Leon Worden.

Advice, suggestions, technical review, and professional assistance were given by James Cornett, Caryn Davidson, Joan Schneider, Paul Smith, Dee Trent, Bill Truesdell, and Claude Warren.

Inspiration was provided by Minerva Hoyt, Linda Greene, and Lary Dilsaver.

My support team at Arcadia Publishing included Jared Nelson, Blake Wright, and Stacia Bannerman. Their help and encouragement was most appreciated.

Lastly, my wife, Marilyn Lutz, lent helpful comments, a listening ear and moral support every step of the way, and my son Tim Zarki created the maps used throughout the book. Thank you, one and all.

INTRODUCTION

In reflecting on the many stories and events surrounding the history of Joshua Tree National Park, one apparent theme emerges. It might best be summed up with the expression "Nothing ever comes easy."

The Joshua Tree region and its peoples engaged in never-ending struggles. The Pinto culture settled in the semiarid Pinto Basin at the end of the Pleistocene epoch and carried out a hunting and gathering lifestyle using atlatls and other early tools. Later Native Americans were semi-migratory, moving from place to place up and down highlands and valleys to follow seasonal foods, making the best of the region's highly arid conditions. Survival sometimes meant conflict with neighbors, as when the Mojave and Chemehuevi fought in 1867, forcing some Chemehuevi to settle at the Oasis of Mara.

Early explorers, such as John C. Frémont, struggled to understand a vast desert that seemed at times both strange and dangerous. Cultural baggage often weighed them down, just as the Romero-Estudillo Expedition in 1823 was hindered by its cumbersome trains of horses, cattle, and pack animals while trying to find a route across the desert to the Colorado River. José Cocomaricopa and his Indian companions traveled light and made the journey with relative ease.

Pioneers in the Joshua Tree area found a land ill-suited to farming, so they sometimes engaged in the time-honored, but illegal, pursuits of cattle rustling, claim jumping, and strong-arming others for land, water, or gold. Even after civilization arrived—much later than most areas—the lives of miners, ranchers, and homesteaders were hard; many pulled up stakes and moved elsewhere. Those who showed flexibility, adaptability, and ingenuity fared better. William and Frances Keys and their family managed to make a home in a secluded, boulder-rimmed valley.

As coastal California began to grow and became more urban, some began to see the desert differently, finding value in its aesthetic appeal, its vast open space, and its strange, intriguing plant and animal life. Minerva Hoyt, Phillip Munz, and Edmund Jaeger fought to preserve the desert. Doing so meant getting others to see value in a place often deemed empty and worthless. That struggle continues today.

Joshua Tree National Monument, far from an idyllic paradise during its early years, battled for survival and recognition, even with its own parent agency. Miners and speculators disregarded President Roosevelt's national monument proclamation and pursued short-term exploitation of the area over long-term preservation.

Today, Joshua Tree National Park enjoys widespread popularity. It is visited by nearly 1.6 million people annually and enjoys a worldwide reputation for its beauty and its recreational value to climbers, hikers, and artists. The park's story is in some ways like a giant Rorschach test. When you look out across its Joshua trees and creosote vistas, you are really looking into a mirror. How you feel about the desert is a fundamental part of the story of Joshua Tree National Park. It is your story too.

One

FIRST PEOPLES
EARLIEST INHABITANTS OF JOSHUA TREE NATIONAL PARK

Humans require food and water to survive, and at first glance, the parched lands of the Mojave and Colorado Deserts would not suggest conditions favorable to human occupation. Yet people have lived in this seemingly barren wilderness for a long time. The earliest evidence of people in what is now Joshua Tree National Park comes from an unlikely location, the sparsely vegetated Pinto Basin. Its discovery was made by two unlikely people, amateur archeologists Elizabeth and William Campbell.

From a spartan desert dwelling in Twentynine Palms, California, the Campbells set out in the mid-1920s to learn everything they could about the native peoples of their new desert home. With no formal training in archeology, they reached out to the Southwest Museum in Los Angeles for professional guidance and began to identify sites and collect artifacts throughout the area. By the early 1930s, their explorations led them to the remote Pinto Basin, where they made discoveries of an early human culture along an ancient lake or streambed. The sediments there contained not only human artifacts but also fossils of extinct Pleistocene mammals such as camels and horses.

The people of the Pinto culture lived by hunting game with atlatls, or throwing-sticks, as determined by the distinctively worked points the Campbells found. Manos and grinding stones showed that seeds from local plants such as mesquite were also gathered and eaten. Formal papers written by Elizabeth in 1935 and 1936 advanced a new approach to desert archeology that focused on environmental factors shaping human settlement patterns.

Recent work has shown that Pinto culture people lived in the area as early as 9,000 years ago. However, geologic studies by George Jefferson and others showed that remains of Pleistocene mammals were eroded by winds into strata where the Pinto culture artifacts were found.

In more recent times, numerous Native American tribal groups made traditional use of the park's valleys, canyons, and rocky ridges. The Serrano occupied a territory that covered much of the central and western regions of the park and extended to the San Gabriel Mountains and Cajon Pass. The Chemehuevi, linked with tribes along the Colorado River, had a large but sparsely populated homeland that covered much of the eastern Mojave Desert and included parts of the Pinto Basin and Coxcomb Mountains. The Cahuilla people comprised several distinct bands, with the desert Cahuilla living among the palm oases of the Coachella Valley. The Mojave Indians lived in villages along the Colorado River, but they carried out trade with coastal tribes that led to the creation of well-known Indian trails across the desert, including areas within the park.

Local Indian tribes in the Joshua Tree region generally lived in small villages where permanent water and food could be obtained. Clans or family groups would make seasonal forays into the mountains and uplands of the modern park to hunt game and gather seasonal foods such as acorns, pine nuts, and mesquite beans. Homes were mainly brush shelters, although, later on, adobe was sometimes used. Food was stored in baskets and pottery ollas. Trade was carried out among the desert and coastal tribes, and there was some mixing of the various tribes and bands as customs forbade marriage between relatives and certain groups of people. Though traditional territories among the local tribes were known, there was some overlap and common use of the Joshua Tree region based on custom and long-term practice. Native groups that lived in areas with adequate soil and water, such along the Colorado River or west of the California desert, grew crops of melons and squash to supplement their traditional native foods.

Contact with the Spanish and, later, Americans brought irrevocable changes to native peoples. Many Serrano were settled near the Spanish mission at San Gabriel, beginning around 1790, and others were forcibly moved there following an attempted revolt in 1810. One group of Serrano, the Maringa, continued to live in the desert with a principal village at Mara, the site of present-day Twentynine Palms and the headquarters of Joshua Tree National Park. It is not known when the Serrano first settled at the Oasis of Mara, but following a smallpox epidemic around 1860, the Serrano largely left the area.

The Chemehuevi are the southernmost group of Paiute Indians, and they have long been closely linked with the Mojave Indians along the Colorado River. Some Chemehuevi also lived among the Halchidoma in villages along the lower Colorado River. The Chemehuevi are thought to have moved into the Mojave Desert region around 1500 CE, occupying territory formerly used by the Mojave. Conflicts with American settlers, miners, and soldiers sometimes found the Chemehuevi allied with the Mojave in occasional attacks. The pressures brought by the growing American incursions along the Colorado River eventually spurred enmity and a prolonged armed conflict between the Mojave and the Chemehuevi, forcing many Chemehuevi to abandon the Colorado River region around 1867. A number of Chemehuevi relocated to the Oasis of Mara at this time.

In the 1870s, the US government began to identify reservations for the native peoples of Southern California. A number of reservations were created for the Cahuilla and other tribes. The Morongo Reservation was home to Cahuilla and Serrano. Indian agent Clara True operated from the Morongo Reservation, from which she made trips by wagon to visit the Chemehuevi living at Twentynine Palms. Other Coachella Valley reservations established for the Cahuilla included Agua Caliente, Torres-Martinez, Cabazon, and Augustine.

In 1892, the Mission Indian Commission proposed to establish a reservation for the Chemehuevi living at Twentynine Palms. Unfortunately, errors were made in recording the lands on which Indian families lived, so the established reservation omitted lands at the oasis and a cemetery where the Chemehuevi buried their dead. Clara True tried to persuade the government to adjust the reservation boundaries to include lands used by the Chemehuevi, but she was ultimately unsuccessful.

The Willie Boy incident in 1909 led nearly all the remaining Chemehuevi to move away from Twentynine Palms to other reservations. Willie Boy, a Paiute living with Chemehuevi relatives, fell in love with his cousin Carlota, daughter of William Mike (Mike Boniface), a Twentynine Palms Chemehuevi. The young couple ran away, but Carlota was tracked down by her relatives and brought back to the oasis. Later, while the family was at Gilman Ranch near Banning, California, Willie Boy killed Mike during an argument and fled again into the desert with Carlota. The ensuing manhunt for Willie Boy captured national attention and led to the tragic and mysterious deaths of Carlota and Willie Boy, although some Chemehuevi believed that Willie Boy escaped.

Following this, Jim and Mathilda Pine remained the only native people living at the Oasis of Mara until they moved away in 1913.

Today, real estate, business growth, and Indian gaming have brought a measure of prosperity to some tribal groups in the Joshua Tree region. In an ironic twist, the Twentynine Palms band of the Mission Indians recently opened a new tribal-owned casino on lands adjacent to Joshua Tree National Park, land mistakenly allotted to the Chemehuevi in lieu of their traditional homes.

Elizabeth Warder Crozer and William Henry "Bill" Campbell met during World War I, and they married in 1920 against the wishes of Elizabeth's family. While serving in Italy, Bill suffered damage to his lungs from mustard gas and was advised to move to the dry desert climate of Twentynine Palms for his health. Their first home was a tent at the Oasis of Mara. (Courtesy of the Twentynine Palms Historical Society.)

Among the Campbells' neighbors was old-timer Bill McHaney. McHaney's deep knowledge of the desert and his friendship with many local Indians kindled in Elizabeth an interest in artifacts and Indian culture. As she later wrote, "As he talked, there was born in my husband and me a great dream of finding 'Indian things' and making a collection of artifacts that would be worthy of some corner in a museum."

With no prior training, the Campbells began a career as amateur archeologists. Through the Southwest Museum in Los Angeles, they began working with archeologists Charles Amsden and Edwin Walker (left). Elizabeth wrote, "Slowly we are learning not to do dumb things, and always we make notes remembering when and where each thing was recovered. When we do not understand the significance of what we see, we leave it undisturbed for better heads than ours."

In the early 1930s, the Campbells began working in the remote Pinto Basin. Here, they discovered numerous archeological sites with sediments that suggested an ancient stream or river flowed through the area. Elizabeth proposed that through the study of environmental features such as topography and water sources, artifacts could be placed in correct chronological relationships. Her theory was bold and unconventional, given her lack of experience, but it eventually gained wide acceptance among archeologists.

When the Campbells began their surveys in the Twentynine Palms region, virtually no archeological work had been done in the California desert. Their studies took them far from most homesteading and mining areas, often into the most isolated desert locales. Field camps were spartan affairs, but the excitement of making new discoveries provided motivation. The Campbells' Pinto Basin work was published in *Southwest Museum Papers* No. 9 in 1935.

During the 1920s, the Campbells concentrated their fieldwork in the area around Twentynine Palms, gradually extending their surveys into more outlying desert areas. They uncovered a great many artifacts, including manos (pestles), metates (mortars), points, pottery, beads, petroglyphs, and pictographs. Bedrock mortars indicated an area of prolonged use. Bill McHaney advised them that whenever they found "grindholes," there were apt to be other artifacts nearby.

The Campbells found petroglyphs and pictographs in many of the areas they surveyed. Petroglyphs have long intrigued desert dwellers. While some figures are representational and depict animals or people, many others are abstract designs. Some authorities have credited petroglyphs to recent Native American tribes, but others have suggested that the rock art is much older, predating modern tribal groups.

When Elizabeth lamented to Bill McHaney that she had found many artifacts, but no ollas, McHaney noted, "There's lots of ollas about, the only trouble is you don't look in the right place!" Eventually, with McHaney's help, the Campbells located many fine ollas. A significant portion of the Campbells' field collections, papers, and photographs are now preserved as part of Joshua Tree National Park's permanent museum collection.

While Elizabeth analyzed their data and formulated many of the ideas laid out in their published papers, Bill Campbell coordinated the logistics for their trips and made many important discoveries. Elizabeth observed, "Mr. Campbell has developed an almost sixth sense of knowing where to look for things, a feeling that . . . would send him diving into a dark hole to return with a treasure in his arms."

The Pinto Basin involved complex problems of geology and paleontology, and the Campbells enlisted the help of scientists from the California Institute of Technology. Dr. Charles Stock and Lawrence Bolles analyzed the animal fossils they found, while David Scharf worked on the stratigraphy of the sediments and volcanic deposits in the area. Here, Bill Campbell looks on as Charles Amsden, a research associate of the Southwest Museum and a longtime collaborator on their studies, uncovers an artifact with a brush.

As their collections grew in size and scope, the Campbells persuaded the Southwest Museum to create a museum branch at Twentynine Palms where artifacts could be stored, studied, and shown to the public. In recognition of their work and their creation of the Desert Laboratory of the Southwest Museum at Twentynine Palms, the museum elected the Campbells as fellows in archeology in 1932.

Elizabeth published a number of important articles and monographs during her lifetime. Many of her papers continue to be cited today, and she established a lasting legacy as a pioneering figure in California desert archeology. Bill Campbell was elected to the Southwest Museum's board of trustees in 1938, but he died in a boating accident in 1944. The Campbell home remains an important local landmark in Twentynine Palms.

The Mojave lived primarily along the Colorado River, where they farmed, hunted, and gathered local plants. They also engaged in active trading with other tribes all the way to the Pacific Coast. Mojave runners, like Panambono and Mitiwara pictured here in 1871, followed established trails across the desert, carrying news and exchanging goods with other tribes. It is likely that Mojave traders passed through the Joshua Tree area on their journeys. (Photograph by Timothy O'Sullivan, courtesy of the Library of Congress.)

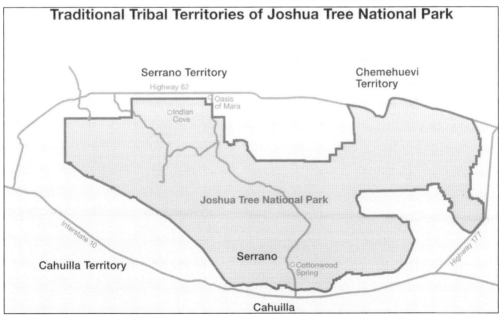

Joshua Tree National Park lies at a crossroads of traditional use areas for the Serrano, Chemehuevi, and Cahuilla peoples. Most use of the park was seasonal in nature, excepting the Serrano village of Mara at present-day Twentynine Palms. Native peoples, usually in small bands of family groups, made temporary encampments in the park to hunt game and gather plants. (Map by Timothy Zarki, original map courtesy of the NPS.)

The name Serrano comes from the Spanish word for mountaineer and refers to several tribes of native peoples that occupied mountainous regions of Southern California. The Tejon Serrano, also called Kitanemuk, lived in the Tejon Creek area near present-day Tehachapi and the western Mojave Desert. By the 1850s, most Serrano bands had settled near missions or on reservations where they experienced hardship, disease, and loss of cultural identity. (Courtesy of the Library of Congress, Edward Curtis Collection.)

The Maringa Serrano was a large Serrano clan centered around Mission Creek and the Morongo Valley area. In the desert area near Joshua Tree, Serrano people lived in pole and brush homes, and they practiced farming, ranching, and traditional hunting and gathering. Maringa leader John Morongo is shown here with his family at their home near Morongo Valley. Morongo was born in 1846 and became a well-known and respected Serrano leader. The US Indian Bureau selected him to serve as a tribal interpreter. (Courtesy of the Twentynine Palms Historical Society.)

The Chemehuevi people once occupied a territory that stretched from the east side of the Colorado River to the San Bernardino Mountains. Characterized as a proud, confident people, Chemehuevi readily mixed with other tribes and have often lived among the Mojave, Halchidoma, Serrano, and Cahuilla. Chemehuevi call themselves Nüwü, or "the People." (Courtesy of the Library of Congress, Edward Curtis Collection.)

Basketmaking was a highly developed craft among the Chemehuevi. Baskets were used for food storage, cooking, and even carrying water. Shown here in 1903, a Chemehuevi woman photographed by George Wharton James demonstrates her skill with openness and good humor. (Courtesy of Holdings of Special Collections and Archives, UCR Libraries, University of California, Riverside.)

The mano and metate have been a feature of native culture in the Joshua Tree region dating back to the Pinto culture. These simple and effective tools were used by all California desert tribes. Native plant foods such as acorns and mesquite beans required grinding. Cakes were made for storage, and mesquite flour was mixed with water to make a nutritious drink. Many native foods compare favorably with modern grains for nutritional value. (Courtesy of Holdings of Special Collections and Archives, UCR Libraries, University of California, Riverside.)

Like their Serrano and Cahuilla neighbors, Chemehuevi built pole and brush structures of several different designs. Some structures were built as homes, while others were used for ceremonies. A temporary dome-shaped hut called a *maha* was built when traveling or hunting. More permanent homes were made of stronger materials, such as adobe. Cooking was often done outside over an open fire or in a cooking pit. (Courtesy of the Library of Congress, Edward Curtis Collection.)

In 1864, the Chemehuevi became involved in a bloody conflict with the Mojave, their onetime allies. Afterward, some Chemehuevi families moved to the Oasis of Mara. Previously a Serrano village, Mara was occupied mostly by Chemehuevi when Bill McHaney arrived there to settle in 1879. In this 1897 image, Chemehuevi women are working on baskets while caring for their young children. (Courtesy of the Twentynine Palms Historical Society.)

Clara True was appointed the Indian agent for the area in 1908, and she may have been the first agent to visit Twentynine Palms. She made trips to the Oasis of Mara in 1909 and 1910. Here, she is buying eggs from Chuck Warren at the Warren Ranch of Yucca Valley in May 1909. Pictured from left to right are William "Pussyfoot" Johnson, Warren, True, Horace Bryan, and his sister Mary from Redlands, California. (Photograph by Maud Russell, courtesy of the Twentynine Palms Historical Society.)

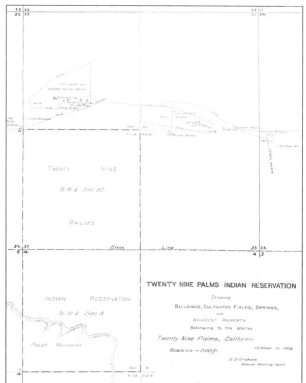

A reservation for the Serrano had been established at Twentynine Palms as early as 1856, but it was never clear what lands were within reservation boundaries. True arranged for a survey of the reservation and found that the oasis and cemetery were outside of the described reservation boundaries. Native Americans living at Mara had no clear title to their ancestral lands even though the reservation was created for their benefit. (Courtesy of the National Archives.)

Shown here in May 1909 are Mike Boniface and his wife, Maria, at their Oasis of Mara home. Mike and Maria were the parents of Carlota, the young Chemehuevi woman who was abducted by Willie Boy. Willie Boy killed Mike just months after this photograph was taken. Mike is credited in some accounts with the discovery of the Desert Queen Mine. (Courtesy of the Twentynine Palms Historical Society.)

Willie Boy, a Paiute adopted by the Twentynine Palms Chemehuevi, fell in love with his cousin Carlota, the teenage daughter of Mike and Maria Boniface. They ran away together from the oasis and were brought back by family and told to stay apart. In September 1909, Willie Boy killed Mike Boniface at Gilman Ranch and escaped into the desert with Carlota, touching off a highly publicized manhunt ending in their deaths. Pursued by a mounted posse (shown below), Willie Boy and Carlota fled in a 600-mile trek northwest of the park before both were found dead. Much uncertainty still surrounds the Willie Boy incident despite several books and a popular Robert Redford film recounting the story. (Both, courtesy of Holdings of Special Collections and Archives, UCR Libraries, University of California, Riverside.)

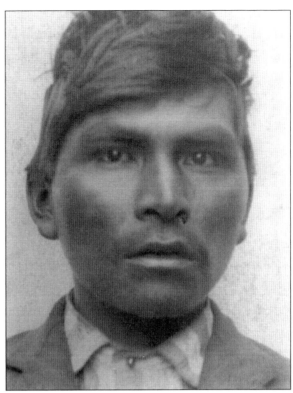

The Willie Boy matter ultimately led to the departure of the Chemehuevi from Twentynine Palms. In anguish over the tragic deaths and the resulting notoriety, the Chemehuevi also faced a 1908 order requiring them to enroll their children at Indian schools in Banning. Rather than be separated from their children, most Chemehuevi moved to reservations at Morongo or Mission Creek. (Courtesy of Holdings of Special Collections and Archives, UCR Libraries, University of California, Riverside.)

Jim Pine was a Serrano leader who lived at the Oasis of Mara with his Cahuilla wife, Mathilda. He facilitated the settlement of the Chemehuevi at the oasis in the late 1860s, following their war with the Mojave. The Pines showed Clara True the graves of their 13 children, buried at the Indian cemetery near the oasis. Jim Pine became leader, or captain, of the Twentynine Palms Chemehuevi following the death of Jim Boniface in 1903. (Courtesy of the Twentynine Palms Historical Society.)

The Cahuilla have lived in the same general area of Southern California for at least 2,000 years. The desert Cahuilla lived among the palm oases of the Coachella Valley and fished along the shores of ancient Lake Cahuilla, near the present Salton Sea. There, the Cahuilla survived with a hunting and gathering lifestyle. Seen above at right, Lee Arenas has just killed a rabbit while his wife, Lupe, holds a basket of mesquite beans. (Left, courtesy of the Library of Congress, Edward Curtis Collection; right, courtesy of Agua Caliente Cultural Museum.)

Cahuilla men typically made large, heavy baskets for food gathering and storage. The finely coiled decorative baskets that were used in ceremonies, as trade goods, and for household use were made by women. Dolores Patencio made baskets of traditional materials such as deer grass and juncus with animals and native plant motifs in their designs. (Courtesy of Agua Caliente Cultural Museum.)

Chief Cabezon was a 19th-century Cahuilla leader of the Agua Caliente who lived near present-day Indio, California. He was recognized by the Mexican government in California as chief of the Cahuilla from San Gorgonio Pass east through the desert regions of the Coachella Valley. Cabezon worked to build good relationships with the Americans, even as the Cahuilla lost lands and population to disease. The town of Cabazon and the Cabazon Reservation are named for him. (Courtesy of Holdings of Special Collections and Archives, UCR Libraries, University of California, Riverside.)

Katherine Siva Saubel was a respected Cahuilla elder and tribal leader who was recognized for her efforts to preserve the Cahuilla language, ceremonies, and customs. She published numerous books in her lifetime, including a Cahuilla-language dictionary and *Temalpakh*, a Cahuilla ethnobotany text. Born on the Los Coyotes Reservation, she lived in her later years at the Morongo Reservation, where she was active in helping establish the Malki Museum. (Courtesy of Agua Caliente Cultural Museum.)

Two

EARLY EXPLORATIONS
THE DESERT IS SLOWLY REVEALED

For a place as popular as Joshua Tree National Park is today, prior to the mid-19th century, its rugged hills and desert valleys remained largely unknown to any but its Native American inhabitants. Though the Spanish penetrated the California desert as early as 1540, direct knowledge of the Joshua Tree region remained elusive and was often shrouded in misconceptions and legends.

One persistent legend concerns the pearl ship of Juan de Iturbe, alleged to have sailed into the ancient Lake Cahuilla by means of a tidal bore in 1615. When the waters receded, the ship was stranded, forcing Iturbe and his crew to make their way out of the desert on foot. If true, this unlikely voyage would have brought Iturbe within sight of the southern boundary of the present park.

Following the establishment of the first missions in California, Pedro Fages, a commander of Spanish forces, led a party north in 1772 from the Spanish presidio at San Diego to capture deserters. While the fugitives escaped, Fages journeyed as far north as Cajon Pass, where he passed through stands of what he thought were date palms, perhaps the first written account of Joshua trees.

Spanish colonial officials wanted to link the newly established missions in Alta California to existing settlements in Arizona and Mexico. Juan Batista de Anza led an expedition across the Colorado Desert in 1774 and returned the following year with more than 240 soldiers and colonists who founded a new settlement at San Francisco Bay. Fr. Francisco Garcés, a member of both expeditions, later made his way up the Colorado River to make contact with and convert the region's Indian tribes. He befriended the Mojave, Chemehuevi, and Serrano tribes, and they guided him along Indian trails that later became the Mojave Road.

In 1821, Mexico declared its independence from Spain, and the new government sought to exert control over Alta California. Hostilities with the Yuma Indians prompted Mexican officials to look for a route from San Gabriel Mission to the Colorado River via San Gorgonio Pass and the Coachella Valley. Capt. Jose Romero and Lt. Jose Estudillo, with a detachment of soldiers, left San Gabriel on December 15, 1823, en route to the Colorado River, but they became lost somewhere north of Desert Center within sight of the lower Pinto Basin and the Coxcomb Mountains along the park's present southeast boundary. Forced to retreat back to San Gabriel Mission, Romero made a second trip and succeeded in reaching the Colorado River in December 1825. However, it was determined the route was impractical.

Fur trappers Jedediah Smith Ewing Young and Kit Carson crossed the Mojave Desert between 1826 and the early 1830s along the trail Garcés followed. Among these early mountain men was Powell "Paulino" Weaver. An associate of Carson, Weaver guided the Mormon Battalion to California during the Mexican War and received a land grant in San Gorgonio Pass. He befriended the local Indians, and they showed him a route to the Colorado River that ascended the mountains via Morongo Valley and struck east to the river by way of the Oasis of Mara. Weaver became the first non-Indian to reach the Morongo Basin, although the exact path of his route to the Colorado River was kept secret.

With the Treaty of Guadalupe Hildalgo and the Gadsden Purchase in 1854, the whole of Alta California became part of the United States, and the government sought to link the newly acquired lands and its goldfields to the rest of the country through a transcontinental railway system. From 1853 to 1855, the US War Department carried out a series of railroad surveys along parallels of latitude to determine the best routes for future rail lines. Lt. Robert S. Williamson was charged with surveying routes in the Southwest to find locations for rail travel from the Gila River drainage across the Colorado River into Central and Southern California. Assisted by Lt. J.G. Parke, geologist William Blake, and other scientists and engineers, Williamson surveyed the southern Sierra Nevada, the Coast Ranges, and the vast deserts east to the Colorado River. It was Lieutenant Parke and William Blake who traveled through San Gorgonio Pass, explored the Cahuilla villages of the Coachella Valley, and journeyed to the Colorado River via the Salton Basin.

Based on Parke's report, Williamson later wrote the first account of the country north of the Coachella Valley: "A mountain range extends from San Bernardino mountain in a southeasterly direction, nearly if not quite to the Colorado. Between these mountains on the Mohave nothing is known of the country. I have never heard of a white man who had penetrated it."

Following the 35th parallel, the survey led by Lt. Amiel Weeks Whipple focused on science and ethnology and provided a wealth of information about Indian tribes along the Colorado River, including the Mojave and the Chemehuevi. The Whipple survey also collected information on plants, animals, and fossils of the region. Although the party did not come close to the Little San Bernardino Mountains, botanist John Bigelow collected the first scientific specimens of the Joshua tree. Both surveys provided illustrations, descriptions, and specimens that added much knowledge about the vast, inaccessible deserts of California.

Finally, on February 24, 1855, Col. Henry Washington, working for the General Land Office, visited the Oasis of Mara. Washington, a contract surveyor, had established the initial point for the San Bernardino Meridian three years earlier. Of his visit to the oasis he noted, "an Indian wigwam . . . and a small cluster of Cabbage Palmetto." A year later, another surveyor, A.P. Green, also visited the oasis and provided a fuller description of the area, "There are a number of fine springs . . . near the springs the land has the appearance of having been cultivated by Indians. There are a few Indian huts in Section 33." Green called the oasis "Palm Springs." Published reports by the federal government and surveyors like Washington and Green began to stir curiosity about the desert. On a visit to Los Angeles in July 1855, Washington was "bombarded with questions about the region lying between the San Bernardino Mountain and the Colorado."

Legends about the desert persist to this day. One unresolved mystery concerns when the common name of Joshua tree first came into popular usage. The name is often credited to Mormon pioneers in the 1850s who encountered the unusual plant and were reminded of the Biblical Joshua. However, no mention of "Joshua tree" has been found in journals kept by Mormon travelers, and accounts by government surveyors and botanists refer to it as a tree yucca or palm.

It would not be until after the Civil War that concerted efforts would be made to penetrate the remote, rugged highlands lying north of the Coachella Valley. As familiar as the region is today, the desert was slow to give up its secrets to the modern world.

In 1769, Pedro Fages arrived at San Diego as military commander. Seeking to recapture several deserters from the Spanish garrison, Fages chased the escapees north and entered the Mojave Desert near Cajon Pass in 1772. He noted passing through groves of date palms, a likely reference to Joshua trees. In 1781, while serving in Sonora, Fages put down a Quechan (Yuma) Indian revolt that had closed the de Anza Trail from Sonora to the California missions. (Courtesy of SCVHistory. com and Santa Clarita Valley Historical Society.)

Father Garcés was a tireless traveler who explored the Colorado River region, establishing contact with the area's Native American tribes. With the help of Mojave guides, he became the first nonnative to cross the desert and reach the coastal missions. His route of travel along the Mojave River became known as the Mojave Road. Father Garcés founded two churches near Yuma Crossing, but he was killed in July 1781 during a Yuma Indian revolt.

Seeking a more direct and safer route to the Colorado River, Capt. Jose Romero and Lt. Jose Estudillo sought to follow the Cocomaricopa Trail, an Indian route that tracked north of the de Anza Trail. However, in early January 1824, their guides became hopelessly lost near the Coxcomb Mountains (shown here) somewhere north of Desert Center. Their initial failure brought the expedition closer to the park than any previous exploration.

Paulino Weaver was a mountain man, trapper, scout, prospector, rancher, and a figure connected with a number of significant events in the frontier history of the Southwest. Apart from being the first nonnative known to visit the Morongo Basin, he also discovered gold near Wickenburg and is credited as the first citizen of Prescott, Arizona. His Weaver Road to the Colorado River likely followed Indian trails, although the exact route was long a mystery. (Courtesy of the Sharlot Hall Museum and Library.)

In April 1844, John C. Frémont, the famous explorer, military officer, and politician, offered an early and rather harsh opinion of the Joshua trees he encountered in the Mojave Desert. Frémont observed, "We were struck by the sudden appearance of yucca trees . . . which gave a strange and southern character to the country, and suited well with the dry and desert region we were approaching . . . their stiff and ungraceful form makes them to the traveller the most repulsive tree in the vegetable kingdom." (Courtesy of the Library of Congress.)

Robert Williamson's career included service in the Navy, a later appointment to West Point, and assignment to the Army Corps of Topographic Engineers. His 1856 railroad survey report recognized that a route through San Gorgonio Pass, the Coachella Valley, and the Colorado Desert offered the easiest and least expensive path for a transcontinental railroad. Mount Williamson in the Sierra Nevada is named for him. (Courtesy of the Library of Congress.)

Williamson assigned Lt. John G. Parke to lead the party that investigated San Gorgonio Pass and the desert between it and the Colorado River. It was Parke who pointed out that the wide opening between the high peaks of San Gorgonio and San Jacinto provided the easiest access for a railroad line across California. Lieutenant Parke later surveyed the northwest boundary with British North America and became a Union major general in the Civil War. (Courtesy of the Library of Congress.)

With orders to find the most practical routes for railroads, Williamson and Parke had no reason to explore the rugged desert highlands of the Little San Bernardino Mountains. In the early 1850s, the area's remoteness and the lack of information about it posed the most significant obstacles to its exploration.

Among the scientists who took part in the Williamson survey was geologist William Phipps Blake. It was Blake who called the low desert east of San Gorgonio Pass the Colorado Desert. Though later scientists applied criteria that differed from Blake's, the name Colorado Desert remains in use today. Blake also recorded information on the ancient Lake Cahuilla, the shorelines of which were visible on rocks he found surrounding the Coachella Valley. (Courtesy of the University of Arizona Mineral Museum.)

While the Williamson survey focused on Southern California, Whipple's survey looked for potential railroad routes across the southern Great Plains and Rockies. The Whipple survey also crossed Arizona and the Mojave Desert, tracing a route that followed the future Route 66. Also known as the ethnology survey, the Whipple party studied Indian tribes it encountered and discovered many new plant species. Rising to major general, Whipple was later killed during the Civil War. (Courtesy of the Maine Historical Society.)

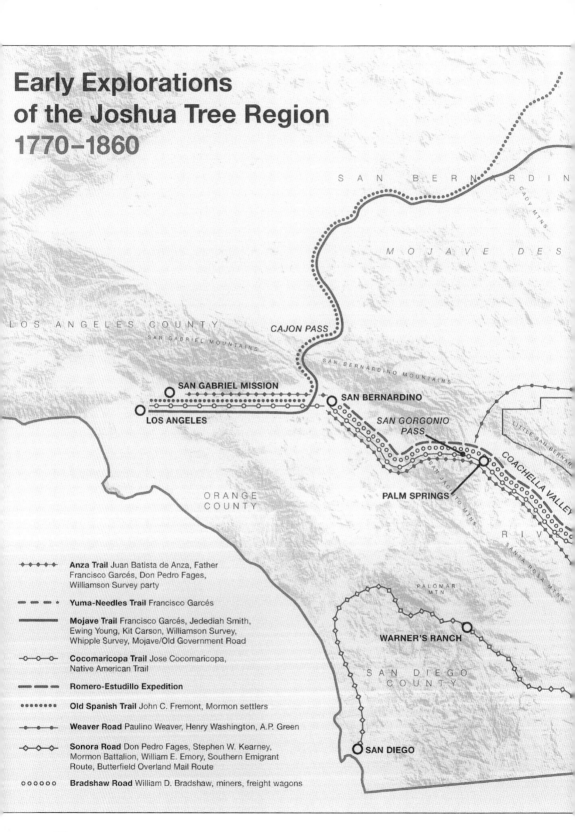

Early Explorations of the Joshua Tree Region 1770–1860

Anza Trail Juan Batista de Anza, Father Francisco Garcés, Don Pedro Fages, Williamson Survey party

Yuma-Needles Trail Francisco Garcés

Mojave Trail Francisco Garcés, Jedediah Smith, Ewing Young, Kit Carson, Williamson Survey, Whipple Survey, Mojave/Old Government Road

Cocomaricopa Trail Jose Cocomaricopa, Native American Trail

Romero-Estudillo Expedition

Old Spanish Trail John C. Fremont, Mormon settlers

Weaver Road Paulino Weaver, Henry Washington, A.P. Green

Sonora Road Don Pedro Fages, Stephen W. Kearney, Mormon Battalion, William E. Emory, Southern Emigrant Route, Butterfield Overland Mail Route

Bradshaw Road William D. Bradshaw, miners, freight wagons

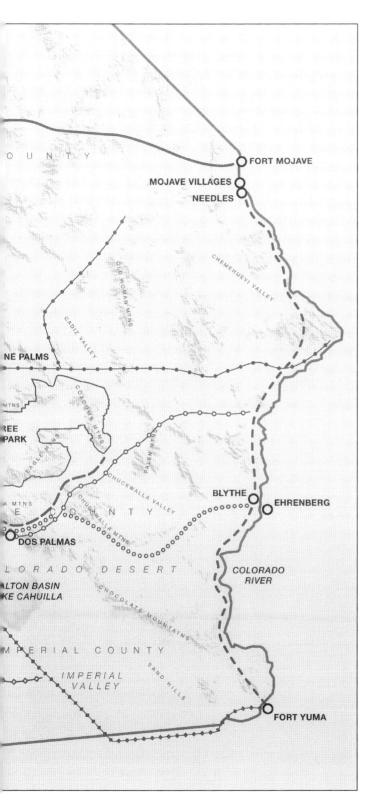

Beginning in the 1770s, the Spanish developed routes of travel across the California desert to support new settlements and missions in Southern California and San Francisco Bay. Often following Native American trails, these routes linked water sources, native villages, and newly developed missions with established settlements in Mexico and Arizona. In the 1800s, fur trappers, Mormon pioneers, and government surveyors expanded knowledge of the desert surrounding Joshua Tree National Park. (Map by Timothy Zarki, derived from an NPS report.)

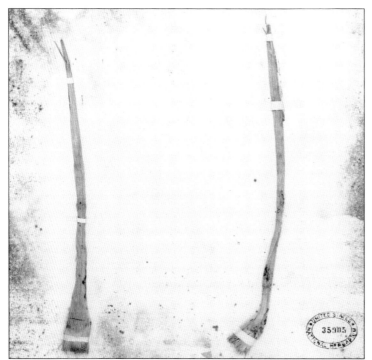

John Milton Bigelow was engaged to serve as the Whipple survey botanist. He obtained the first scientific specimens of the Joshua tree in 1853 and wrote in his report, "In addition to the trees already mentioned, we noticed here vast quantities of the tree Yucca, called by the Mexicans *Palma* . . . it is found here from twenty-five to thirty-five feet in height, and eighteen inches or two feet in diameter, with a bark on the lower part of the trunk very much resembling that of white oak." (Courtesy of the Smithsonian.)

Bigelow collected hundreds of plant specimens, including many desert cacti such as the barrel cactus and saguaro. The striking jumping cholla, the signature plant of the park's Cholla Cactus Garden, is named *Opuntia bigelovii* in his honor. Bigelow's report for the survey also includes many beautiful illustrations of plants encountered on their travels.

Charles Koppel, artist for the Williamson survey, created several striking lithographs of the strange tree encountered by the railroad surveys in the Tejon and Cajon Pass areas. Unlike Frémont, members of the Williamson and Whipple parties were more favorably impressed by the tall, spiky plant. On February 6, 1854, Whipple observed, "Another beautiful addition to the scenery appeared to-day; groves of tall and branching Yucca, with shining leaves, radiating like a wide-spread fan. They are twenty or thirty feet high, with trunks from a foot and a half to two feet in diameter. The leaves grow upon the extremities of the branches, and each year are folded back to give place to a new set. It is in this way that the trunks attain their great size." (Colorplate from *Routes in California, to Connect with the Routes near the Thirty-Fifth and Thirty-Second Parallels, Explored by Lieutenant R. S. Williamson, Corps of Topographical Engineers, in 1853. Geological Report, by William P. Blake, Geologist and Mineralogist of the Expedition.*)

Visits to the Oasis of Mara by land office surveyors Henry Washington in 1855 and A.P. Green in 1856 marked the beginning of the era of white settlement and land use of Joshua Tree National Park. These early surveys provided the first written accounts of future parklands. Green noted the name of the oasis as Palm Springs. By the 1870s, early homesteaders were using "Twenty-nine Palms Springs" as the name for the oasis. (Photograph by Ron Croci and Robert Caughlin III, courtesy of Action 29 Palms.)

Much uncertainty surrounds the story of how the Joshua tree got its name. It is thought that Mormon pioneers named the Joshua tree for its resemblance to the Biblical prophet whose upraised arms beckoned them home to Utah. Mormon settlers from San Bernardino were recalled to Utah in the 1850s. The record is not clear, and the name did not come into widespread use until the 20th century. (Photograph by Burton Frasher, courtesy of the NPS.)

Three

SETTLING IN
AT HOME ON THE RANGE

Though the Gold Rush brought thousands of people to California before the Civil War, it was not until after the war's end that white settlers began to have a lasting impact on the Joshua Tree area. A Jeff Davis mining claim was recorded within the future park in 1865, and the first homesteads were filed at Twentynine Palms in 1873. A mining district was established, and Bill McHaney, a cattleman, arrived and took up residence at the oasis, becoming its first permanent white settler in 1879.

While mining would become the dominant economic activity of the park area, it was cattle that brought the early influx of whites to the region. Grass-covered valleys offering good winter grazing, a handful of springs, and remote canyons made the area attractive for the entrepreneurial cowboy little concerned with the niceties of proper cow ownership. Oliver Smith is reputed to have run Texas longhorns near Quail Springs from 1870 to 1876. Bill McHaney began grazing longhorns in the Keys Ranch area as early as 1879.

Bill McHaney, with his wilder brother Jim and a handful of others, began to operate during the 1880s as the McHaney Gang, running cattle in the Hidden Valley area of the park. Cattle would be driven from southern Arizona to the boulder-strewn valleys of the Little San Bernardino Mountains where they could be easily corralled with little outside notice and then sold to the growing markets of Southern California. Brands were changed at a place known as Cow Camp. Here, wells were dug and several adobe cabins were built to support the McHaney Cow Ranch.

As more established cattle operators began using the area, rustling activities declined. However, cattle were accountable property for cowboys, so it was not an uncommon practice to keep a few unbranded animals hidden away in case some "missing" cows needed to be replaced.

Bill McHaney eventually sold his cattle interests to George Meyers in 1894, and C.O. Barker bought Meyers out in 1905. Barker partnered with Will Shay, and the Barker and Shay Cattle Company ran 200 to 400 head throughout the park.

The Ryan brothers, Jepp and Tom, owners of the Lost Horse Mine, grazed about 100 head of cattle in the Lost Horse and Stubbe Springs areas during the 1890s. They made their headquarters at Lost Horse Well near the base of Ryan Mountain and built an adobe house, bunkhouse, stable, and corrals. The Ryans figure prominently in the park's mining history as owners of the Lost Horse Mine.

Other cattle operators included the Swartout Company based in Twentynine Palms, James Cram and Jerry Wolford, James Stocker, and Katherine "Captain" Barry.

The cattle era left its mark on the park through improvements designed to support grazing operations. Water impoundments, known locally as tanks, were built to provide more reliable water sources for livestock. Barker Dam, Cow Camp, White Tank, and Ivanpah Tank were among the sites connected with grazing operations.

The story of one early settler touches on nearly all aspects of the pioneer experience at Joshua Tree. William F. "Bill" Keys, born George Barth, grew up in Nebraska but moved west as a young man seeking opportunity and perhaps some adventure. He worked as a ranch hand in Colorado, joined Teddy Roosevelt's Rough Riders, changed his name to William Key, worked copper mines in Jerome, Arizona, and was a deputy sheriff for Mojave County before drifting up to Death Valley in 1905 to try his hand at prospecting. At Death Valley, Key located the Desert Hound Mine and became involved with flamboyant prospector and master showman Death Valley Scotty in a mining scheme that went awry, resulting in the accidental shooting of Scott's brother, Warner. Narrowly avoiding arrest, Key sold his Death Valley claims and drifted through California's mining camps before arriving in the Twentynine Palms area about 1910, where he found work as a caretaker and assayer at the Desert Queen Mine.

His work at the Desert Queen Mine led to his acquisition of the old McHaney Ranch, including the rustlers' Cow Camp. Calling it the Desert Queen Ranch, he would make the area his lifelong home. Keys added the s to his name, met and married Los Angeles resident Frances Lawton, and began to raise a family.

For the next 50 years, he would try his hand at virtually every activity that would enable his family to survive in their harsh desert home. He dug wells and built dams to ensure a steady supply of water for his ranch and mining ventures. He filed on numerous old mining claims, often just to get equipment, mining timbers, and spare parts. The Keys family raised livestock, including cattle, chickens, and goats for food. With his horses and mules, Keys hauled ore and supplies to area mines, both his own as well as the claims of others. He set up stamp mills, first at the ranch, and later at Wall Street Mill, where he processed gold ore from the Desert Queen and for other area mines. He learned that he could earn money from leasing his gold claims to others and then processing the excavated ore for a fee.

The family planted fruit trees and raised garden crops and grains for their food, eventually raising enough to sell the excess. With a growing family, Keys established a school at the ranch that his family, as well as those of other miners and ranchers, could attend. The county agreed to provide a teacher, and Keys built a cabin for the teacher's residence.

Keys befriended many of the other miners, including Bill McHaney and Johnny Lang. He eventually acquired the holdings and property of older miners as they either died or left the area, and Keys gradually transformed the ranch into sprawling junkyard of machinery, vehicles, equipment, and spare parts. Nothing was thrown away, and many objects were repurposed and adapted to meet a need. The isolation of the ranch drove the Keys family to constantly adapt and innovate in order to thrive in their remote desert existence. Occasionally, tragedy struck the family, as several children died and were buried on the property in a family cemetery.

Though welcoming to many travelers and older desert residents, Keys fiercely defended his holdings, sometimes using gunplay to settle disputes over water rights and trespass. In 1929, Keys shot and wounded Homer Urton, a Barker and Shay cowboy, over access to a water hole. Keys gained a reputation as a man one did not want to cross. His conflicts with others would eventually lead to tragic consequences later in his life.

The springs at the Oasis of Mara, also called the Palms in the 1870s, attracted wayfarers from the earliest days. Water and shade made it a good camping spot and a natural place to meet others and learn about the surrounding country. During the 1880s, miners set off from the oasis for the new gold discoveries at Dale. The area's earliest homestead claims were filed at the site despite long-established Indian occupation of the area.

C.O. Barker and Will Shay acquired the cattle interests of George Meyers, formerly of the McHaney Gang, in 1905. The Barker and Shay Cattle Company operated within the present-day national park from 1905 to 1923. Barker and Shay drove their cattle up into the Lost Horse Valley area in May and wintered their herds in Morongo Valley. (Courtesy of the Twentynine Palms Historical Society.)

The Talmadge brothers—Will, John, and Frank—had a cattle operation with summer range near Big Bear and winter range extending from Yucca Valley to Mission Creek. In 1909, they bought Warren's Well and used the site for spring roundups. The Talmadges bought the Barker and Shay cattle interest in 1923 and thereafter ran over 400 head of cattle in the park. Here, a Talmadge cowboy drives cattle near Morongo Valley in spring of 1935. (Courtesy of the Twentynine Palms Historical Society.)

Ben de Crevecoeur was part of the first white family to settle in the Morongo Valley area, in 1873. His father settled at what became known as Warren's Ranch. The family ran cattle and sheep between there and Twentynine Palms. Ben later worked as a freight hauler at the Lost Horse Mine and became a sheriff. He and his brother Waldemar were part of the Willie Boy posse in 1909. (Courtesy of the Twentynine Palms Historical Society.)

Mark "Chuck" Warren was a teamster who came to the area in 1881 and dug Warren's Well at present-day Yucca Valley. In 1884, he and his wife, Sylvia, acquired the de Crevecoeur Ranch in Big Morongo Canyon, and it became known as Warren's Ranch. Mark married Sylvia Mae Paine when she was 14, and they ran cattle from the Morongo Valley area through Yucca Valley. (Courtesy of the Twentynine Palms Historical Society.)

Warren's Ranch served as a stop on the stage route from Banning to Dale. The genial Mark Warren and his family welcomed travelers to their home with water and forage. Shown here in 1900 with his family are, from left to right, son-in-law Charlie Reche, daughter Frances Warren Reche holding Warren Reche, Sylvia Mae Warren, Will Warren, Thelma Reche, and Mark Warren. Charlie Reche was also a member of the Willie Boy posse and was wounded during the manhunt. (Courtesy of the Twentynine Palms Historical Society.)

Moving herds from winter range at Lost Horse, Quail Springs, and Barker Dam to summer range in the San Bernardino Mountains, local cattleman often held their roundups at Warren's Well. Animals were branded here, and cattle that were to be sent to market were driven to the railroad at Victorville. With its water and forage, Warren's Well was a key property for the local cattle industry. In 1909, the Talmadge brothers bought the well following Mark Warren's death, and it was acquired by Barker and Shay in 1918. (Courtesy of the Twentynine Palms Historical Society.)

William "Bill" Covington was a foreman for Chase & Law, a Banning cattle company that grazed herds south of Yucca Valley in an area now called Covington Flat, where Covington lived for a number of years. Covington later owned a homestead adjacent to Warren Ranch and ran cattle on open range. He acquired Warren's Ranch in 1917 and built a mill on his ranch to process ore. Morongo Valley's Covington Park is named for him. Also pictured are Covington's wife, Bertha, and their three eldest children—Vaden, Sara, and Leonard. (Courtesy of the Twentynine Palms Historical Society.)

Barker and Shay cowboys take a break at Coyote Wells in 1927. Located in the community of Joshua Tree, Coyote Wells was developed by Barker and Shay in 1915 to support their wide-ranging cattle operations. Pictured here are, from left to right, Gus Seely, unidentified, Frank Urton, unidentified, Albert Urton, and unidentified. Homer Urton, another Barker and Shay cowhand, was wounded by Bill Keys in 1929 after he was caught trespassing on land that Keys claimed. (Courtesy of the Twentynine Palms Historical Society.)

In 1912, C.O. Barker hired Jep Whitney to build a dam at White Tank, shown here in 1936. Bill Keys hauled cement for the job. Access to water was critical for any cattle outfit operating in the desert. With only a few natural springs in the Joshua Tree area, cattlemen built dams and impoundments to create tanks for water storage. Barker and Shay built numerous tanks and wells and acquired water rights throughout the park area.

A low stone wall built by George Meyers and Bill McHaney was the first water development at Barker Dam. In 1902, Barker and Shay built a nine-foot-high dam that was declared a public water reserve in 1914. Bill Keys claimed the area as part of a homestead, but his claim was invalidated. Keys later raised the height of the dam another three feet and called it Bighorn Dam. He carved an inscription in cement at the top. When full, the impounded water creates a six-acre lake.

In the 1880s, Cottonwood Spring became an important stopping point for freight haulers and miners traveling between Mecca and Dale. It was the only reliable spring for many miles. Cattlemen James Cram and Jerry Wolford watered their livestock at the oasis. Water from Cottonwood was pumped to the Iron Chief Mine, 18 miles away. A caretaker lived in a cabin on the site, and writer J. Smeaton Chase found fruit trees and a vegetable garden when he visited Cottonwood in 1919. (Courtesy of the US Geological Survey.)

Ryan Ranch was built by Tom and Jepp Ryan as a base for their mining and cattle operations. Nearby Lost Horse Well supplied water for the Lost Horse Mine and also enabled the Ryans to maintain a herd of 100 cattle. The adobe house was built by Sam Temple in 1896, and gold tailings from the Lost Horse Mine were used to make the bricks so that the walls were said to assay out at $8 a ton. Later, frame and stucco rooms were added to the house. Other structures included a bunkhouse, a root cellar, and corrals. Members of the Ryan family lived there until the early 1940s. A fire in 1978 destroyed the main house, leaving only skeletal walls as a reminder of the ranch's heyday. Ryan Ranch is listed in the National Register of Historic Places.

Ryan Ranch served as a camp for miners working at the Lost Horse Mine. Several graves are found here, but information about them is shrouded in legend and uncertainty. A boulder near Ryan Ranch is said to contain the remains of Frank James, original claimant of the Desert Queen Mine, who was killed by Charlie Martin in a dispute with Jim McHaney over ownership of the mine. Lopes was said to be one of five Mexican miners killed in a brawl.

Desert Queen Ranch was first settled by the McHaneys, who used it for their cattle operation and as a millsite for the Desert Queen Mine. In addition to building a stamp mill, the McHaneys dug a well and built several adobe buildings, including a large barn. When Bill Keys began working at the mine, he also took care of the millsite and began living at the ranch, perhaps as early as 1910. (Photograph by Ross Carmichael, courtesy of Frances Carmichael.)

Bill Keys married Frances May Lawton in 1918, the same year he took ownership of the Desert Queen Ranch and mine. Children came soon after; they are shown here in the late 1920s. From left to right are Willis, Virginia, and Ellsworth. As on most ranches, the children always had chores: hauling water and wood, gathering eggs, and helping their mother can fruits and vegetables in summer. Play consisted of climbing on rocks and fashioning toys from everyday objects.

Frances Lawton Keys was born in Toledo, Ohio, but moved to Los Angeles with her family. She was working at Western Union when she met Bill Keys and moved to the isolated Desert Queen Ranch. She wore sunbonnets to protect her skin and was fond of colored glass, gathering a large collection that she displayed on a table outside their home. Frances's mother and several brothers would often visit the ranch to help with the never-ending work.

Frances Keys was the first teacher for the ranch children. Local miner and mechanic Oran Booth had once taught school, so Bill asked him begin teaching his children at the ranch in 1930. Finally, former missionaries Howard and Della Dudley arrived in 1937 and began providing instruction for the Keys' children, as well as for those of other ranch and mining families. Della was the primary teacher while Howard said morning prayers for the students and helped Bill with chores.

Though not an engineer, Keys applied his energy and ingenuity to building dams at the Desert Queen Ranch, Cow Camp, and at other locations where he had a need for water. Starting in 1914, Keys built three dams at Keys Ranch to create one large impoundment. Keys finished the dam at Cow Camp in 1948. He often used a cable tram taken from the Desert Queen Mine to help with dam construction projects. Keys's dams still hold water today.

Though mining was their main activity, the Keys family farmed crops and raised a wide variety of livestock. In addition to cattle, they kept goats, rabbits, and chickens for food. Horses, mules, and burros helped them get around and haul materials and supplies. The dam behind the main ranch house supplied water for livestock, as well as crops and the stamp mill. Keys filed on or acquired numerous homesteads, ultimately owning about 880 acres of desert land.

A native of Sweden, John Samuelson was a seaman who began working for Bill Keys at the Hidden Gold Mine in 1926. He lived for a while at the Desert Queen Ranch before he filed for a homestead near Quail Springs at the base of a rocky hill. From this lonely outpost, Samuelson spent his time carving numerous boulders with paragraph-long expressions of political commentary and creatively spelled philosophy. Not long after, Samuelson left the desert when his homestead was invalidated because he was a noncitizen. Years later, he killed two men at a dance, was judged insane, and committed to a state hospital. Escaping from there, he made his way to Washington State where, in 1954, he was injured in a logging accident and died.

Erle Stanley Gardner was an attorney, pulp-fiction writer, and desert traveler. Gardner loved nature, and he often drove his custom van to the desert for weekend camping excursions. The van was equipped with a Dictaphone that Gardner used to record stories for later transcription. He occasionally camped among the Joshua trees at Quail Springs, where he met homesteader John Samuelson. Samuelson related a remarkable life story to Gardner, and after paying Samuelson $20 for rights to his tale, Gardner fashioned it into the story "Rain Magic," published by *Argosy* magazine in 1928. Gardner soon became famous as the author of the Perry Mason mysteries. (Both, courtesy of Temecula Valley Museum, City of Temecula.)

Four

Hard Rock
in a Hard Land
The Mining Era

In 1873, Dave Gowen and Joseph Voshay made the initial gold discoveries near Twentynine Palms, and two arrastras and a stamp mill were constructed to process the ore. The Anaconda Mine was one of the earliest mines and thought to have first been worked by a man named Drinkwater, a member of Washington's 1855 survey. Phil Sullivan was a later owner of the Anaconda as well as the nearby Contact Mine, which he developed in 1910 with Bill McHaney. A new quartz mill was developed in town in 1908 to handle increased production from the local mines.

Lew Curtis located rich placer deposits east of Twentynine Palms in 1883, and the tent city of Virginia Dale, later shortened to Dale, quickly arose, reaching a population of perhaps 1,000 people. Two years later, Tom Lyons and Jonathan "Quartz" Wilson found rich quartz veins that were developed as the Virginia Dale Mine. The Virginia Dale, together with other discoveries near the Pinto Basin, spurred the rise of another town of Dale, south along the Gold Crown Road. Development of the Supply Mine around 1900 led to yet another town, New Dale, even farther south and east of the original Dale. The Supply was the richest of the region's mines, and as a result, New Dale supported the largest population of the three Dale communities. The Los Angeles, Brooklyn, OK, and Gold Crown Mines were among the most prosperous of hundreds of claims worked in the area between 1890 and 1920.

Success of the Dale-area mines pushed prospectors ever deeper into the desert, and new mining districts such as the Rattler, Monte Negras, Eagle Mountains, and Cottonwood were soon created. Rail lines reached the distant communities of Amboy to the north and Mecca to the south. From these locations, freight wagons hauled timbers and mining equipment to Dale and other remote mining districts. Cottonwood Spring, with its reliable water, became an important stopping point on the freight route from Mecca to Dale.

The McHaney Gang figured prominently in a number of the region's most significant and colorful mining discoveries. Numerous legends surround the origins of the Lost Horse and Desert Queen Mines. In 1893, John Lang was a young cowboy driving cattle to California from New Mexico. While searching for a lost horse, he encountered Jim McHaney near the Desert Queen Ranch. McHaney threateningly told him the horse was no longer lost. Retreating south toward Witch Spring, Lang encountered Frank "Dutch" Diebold, who had made a rich gold strike nearby, but he too had been driven off by the McHaneys. Lang offered to buy the claim from Diebold, and on the advice of his father, he took on a number of partners. Two years later, Lang and his partners sold their interest to the Ryan family, who started the Lost Horse Mining Company and erected a 10-stamp mill on the site. The Lost Horse Mine became the richest mine in the area, producing more than 10,500 ounces of gold and 8,500 ounces of silver between 1895 and 1908.

Cloudier still are the circumstances surrounding the birth of the Desert Queen Mine. A miner named James, possibly Frank L. James, began working the Desert Queen area as early as 1892. Shortly afterwards, he became embroiled in a dispute with the McHaney Gang over claim markers they had located on top of James's discovery. A violent argument ensued, and James was killed by Charles Martin, allegedly in self-defense after Martin claimed James attacked him with a knife.

Other versions had Bill McHaney filing the claim in January 1895 after learning about it from Twentynine Palms Chemehuevi Mike Boniface. Or it was Jim McHaney who made the discovery while running cattle. Whatever the truth, the Desert Queen Mine began production in 1895 and soon produced rich yields. A five-stamp mill was built at the Desert Queen Ranch to process the ore. Outside investors were brought in as Jim McHaney's lavish lifestyle quickly exhausted operating capital for the mine. Over the next decade, the Desert Queen passed through a variety of owners and partners before coming into the hands of mining engineer William Morgan.

Morgan hired Bill Keys in 1910 to be a caretaker at the mine. Keys worked the mine for a number of years, often without wages, and took care of the mine's equipment and machinery. With Morgan's death in 1917, Keys became owner of the mine and its associated properties, including the old McHaney Ranch headquarters, later called the Desert Queen Ranch. From 1895 through 1941, the Desert Queen produced more than 3,800 ounces of gold worth several million dollars.

Around 1901, James "Chuckwalla Jim" Wilson found gold stringers in a boulder in the Hexie Mountains. When rock samples were processed, they yielded $500 worth of gold. Wilson named his strike the El Dorado. However, Wilson did not actively develop the claim and sold it in 1903. Little happened at the site until 1907, when new investors formed the El Dorado Consolidated Mining Company. With Fred Vaile as superintendent, the El Dorado produced handsomely throughout World War I. The El Dorado closed in 1922 only to reopen a year later under lease to John White. At its peak, a 10-stamp mill worked the gold ore, and water was piped from Pinyon Well nine miles away. When production ceased in the late 1930s, over 2,000 ounces of El Dorado gold had been recovered.

Perhaps the richest mineral discovery in the Joshua Tree region involved not the precious metals of gold and silver, but the more utilitarian iron. A prospector named Joe Torres left some ore samples at the store in Mecca. Mining engineer L.S. Barnes found the samples and recognized them as rich in iron ore. In 1892, Barnes located numerous claims in the Eagle Mountains, and William Stevens and Thomas Doffelmeyer located the Iron Chief Mine. Charles Lane bought the mine in 1897 and produced gold from the site. Water was supplied by pipeline from Cottonwood Spring, 18 miles away. Lane was unable to make payments on the site, and the property reverted to the original owners. Barnes purchased an option on the Iron Chief claims and sold them in 1912 to E.H. Harriman, president of the Southern Pacific Railroad. The Iron Chief lay dormant until 1944, when Southern Pacific sold the claims to the Henry J. Kaiser Corporation, thereby setting the stage for the park's largest environmental controversy. Kaiser proceeded to develop the Eagle Mountain Mine, one of the largest iron mines in the western United States.

When Bill McHaney took up residence at Twentynine Palms in 1879, he was the first non-Indian to settle there. Though cattle ranching with his brother took up most of his early years, McHaney became a prospector and miner. After he sold his cattle interests and lost the Desert Queen Mine, McHaney spent many years at a rustic mining camp in the Music Valley area searching for a rich strike.

Jonathan "Quartz" Wilson was an early prospector and resident at the Twentynine Palms oasis. During his life, Wilson made numerous mining discoveries. In 1885, he located the Virginia Dale Mine with Thomas Lyons. He later discovered the North Star Mine. Like many prospectors, Wilson found the search for gold more appealing than the actual mining of it. (Courtesy of the Van Lahr Collection.)

Quartz Wilson came to Twenynine Palms around 1883, and he settled at the Oasis of Mara. He lived in a dugout house built into the side of a hill with his dog Sniff and a cat. Years earlier, Wilson had discovered a rich silver lode in the desert somewhere northeast of Twentynine Palms. Despite the help of several experienced miners, he was never able to relocate his "Lost Wilson Mine." (Courtesy of the Van Lahr Collection.)

Phil Sullivan arrived in the Twentynine Palms area in 1897 and was a key figure in the development of the area's mines. Sullivan was the owner of the Anaconda and Contact Mines for many years. In 1910, Sullivan and Bill McHaney built an arrastra at the Palms. Apart from his own mines, Sullivan was a blacksmith and performed assessment and caretaker work for a number of area mines. (Photograph by Harlow Jones, courtesy of the Van Lahr Collection.)

The Anaconda Mine is considered one of the oldest mines in Joshua Tree National Park. It was said to have been located by a member of the Washington survey party. By 1907, it was owned by the Taylor-Sullivan Mining Company, who leased it to Edward MacDermott. MacDermott, shown standing by the upper tank in 1916, and his partners built a quartz mill in Twentynine Palms to process the ore. (Courtesy of the Van Lahr Collection.)

Following its discovery in 1885, the Virginia Dale Mine began operation a year later, using a five-stamp mill. Water was pumped to the site from the mining town of Dale. Operating costs were high, and the mine was periodically inactive. A second five-stamp mill was moved to the Virginia Dale in 1896, when the original mill was supposedly buried in a sandstorm. The Virginia Dale operated intermittently up until World War II and produced about $200,000 in ore.

The Supply Mine was the richest mine in the Dale mining district. Located by Frank Sabathe, it was initially operated by the Seal of Gold Mining Company. From 1911 to 1915, the mine was leased by the United Greenwater Copper Company, which expanded the mill's capacity to 100 tons. The mine employed more than 80 workers, and it led to the rise of the town of New Dale.

In 1893, John Burt and F.J. Botsford discovered several mines in the Dale mining district. The Brooklyn Mine, the Los Angeles Mine, and the OK Mine were all notable producers. Ore from the Brooklyn was initially milled at the town of Dale, but two three-stamp mills were later erected at the Brooklyn Mine. Water was hauled all the way from Cottonwood Spring. In 1899, the Brooklyn Mine was sold to new owners who established the Brooklyn Mining Company and operated the site until about 1916. (Courtesy of the Twentynine Palms Historical Society.)

Due to their proximity, the Los Angeles and Brooklyn Mines were operated jointly and used a common mining camp, shown here in 1920. Judge John Campbell of the Campbell Gold Lease Company took a 25-year lease on the Brooklyn and Los Angeles properties in 1921. Ore was taken to the Gold Crown Mill for processing. Mine records show that 3,497 ounces of gold and 2,845 ounces of silver were recovered from the mines prior to 1930. (Courtesy of the Twentynine Palms Historical Society.)

Rail lines came only as close to the Joshua Tree mining districts as Mecca to the south and Amboy to the north. To reach the mining areas of Dale and Twentynine Palms, mine timbers, equipment, and many supplies had to be hauled by heavy freight wagons; trips took three to five days. Here, Jim Grier drives a wagon team from Amboy to Dale. Amboy Crater is visible in the background. (Photograph by Maud Russell, courtesy of the Van Lahr Collection.)

Shown here is the third town of Dale, about 1911–1912. Spurred by the development of the Supply Mine and the backing of financier Charles Schwab's United Greenwater Copper Company, the last Dale had the largest population of the three Dale communities. It was situated about six miles south of the earlier towns, close to the OK and Supply Mines, the area's largest producers. The town prospered until about 1917, when mining activity ceased. (Courtesy of the Van Lahr Collection.)

The Dale pumping station was critical to the town, as it pumped water to the nearby mines for ore processing. Shown here in 1912 are, from left to right, pumper Julius Ellerman, stage driver Johnny Castaigne, and an unidentified passenger. The area's mining activity prompted the county to improve roads to the area in the late 1890s, allowing stage lines to bring passengers to Dale. One-way fare from Palm Springs was $11. (Courtesy of the Van Lahr Collection.)

A wagon trip to Dale was arduous under any circumstances, but for Maria Whallon, it proved especially tragic. Maria's mother had accepted a position as a cook at the Dale mines. She brought along her 18-year-old daughter, sick with tuberculosis, hoping that Maria's health would improve in the desert climate. However, the rigors of the long wagon trip proved fatal, and Maria died in March 1903. She was buried by Phil Sullivan at the Oasis of Mara. (Courtesy of the Van Lahr Collection.)

Pictured here, Phil Sullivan (left) and Al Vivian return to Twentynine Palms around 1915–1916 after hauling ore to the mill at the El Dorado Mine. Sullivan and Vivian located the Silver Bell Mine in 1923, "1-1/2 miles Southeasterly from Anaconda Mine." Later, other mines also named Silver Bell were located by Sullivan and others. Today, a mine called the Silver Bell is featured in a park exhibit along the Pinto Basin Road, miles away from the original mine. (Courtesy of the Van Lahr Collection.)

In 1893, John "Johnny" Lang located the Lost Horse Mine, a property that would become the area's richest gold producer. After selling out to the Ryans in 1896, Lang operated the night shift at the mill. The Ryans soon discovered that ore produced at night was consistently less than the day-shift production. Caught stealing gold amalgam, Lang was given a choice—sell out for $12,000 or go to jail. Lang took the money and moved to a nearby canyon that now bears his name. (Courtesy of the Twentynine Palms Historical Society.)

Johnny Lang filed for location of the Lost Horse Mine with his father, George, and partners Ed Holland and James Fife. Work began immediately, and a two-stamp mill was built. In this 1893 photograph, freight teams at the Lost Horse Well millsite haul materials and supplies for the new mine. Ben de Crevecoeur is the second team driver from the right. (Courtesy of the Twentynine Palms Historical Society.)

Thomas Ryan (pictured in 1935), along with family members Jepp, Matthew, Ethan, and Samuel Kelsey, purchased the Lost Horse Mine in 1896. Johnny Lang retained a minority ownership in the new Lost Horse Mining Company. The Ryans erected the 10-stamp mill at the mine site and built a 3.5-mile pipeline from Lost Horse Well to the mine.

The years 1895–1908 saw peak production at the Lost Horse Mine, with operations yielding large quantities of gold and silver. Improvements at Ryan Ranch in support of the mine included an assay office, cookhouse, and bunkhouse. After 1912, the mine was often shut down, although occasional upgrades were made, such as replacing steam-powered equipment with gas. Though the Ryans sold the Lost Horse Mine in 1912, they held operational control of the property into the 1930s.

After selling out his stake in the Lost Horse Mine, Johnny Lang moved to a nearby canyon that now bears his name. He lived in a cabin and milled a small amount of ore from a new mine, the Sulfide-Bismuth Mine. After the Lost Horse Mine shut down, Lang moved back and lived at the mine. According to Bill Keys, Lang returned to the Lost Horse Mine to recover some of the gold amalgam he had buried. Lang lived a hermit-like life, and his health declined. One day in January 1925, he left a note on his cabin saying, "Gone to town for supplies, will be back soon." Keys (at left) found Lang's body on March 22 near the road he was building to his Hidden Gold Mine. He returned three days later with Jeff Peeden (at right) and Frank Kiler and buried Lang where he was found. (Both, courtesy of the Twentynine Palms Historical Society.)

The Pinyon Well Mill was developed by Alfred Tingman and Ed Holland to process ore from the Pinyon Mine and other claims in the Pinyon mining district. A two-stamp mill operated in the area as early as 1890. Because there was water, the mill processed ore for several notable mines, including the Lost Horse and Desert Queen Mines. Several families with children lived there from 1895 until the mill closed in 1918.

Located near Pleasant Valley, the Hexahedron "Hexie" Mine was prospected by Ed Holland and Al Tingman in 1894. Up to 12 men were working the gold claims in 1907. Shown here in 1911, Bill Garrison (center) bought the Hexie Mine with Quartz Wilson (left) and formed the Hexahedron Mining Company. Work at the Hexie Mine stopped around 1918. (Courtesy of the Van Lahr Collection.)

Despite its discovery in 1901, development of the El Dorado Mine was slow at first. Former clergyman John White acquired the claims from Chuckwalla Wilson in 1903 and built a camp, but he was unable to erect a mill. When the El Dorado Consolidated Mining Company took over the property in 1907, it was renamed the New El Dorado Mine. Shafts were dug, and the first production of gold and silver occurred in 1911. (Courtesy of the Twentynine Palms Historical Society.)

Bill Taylor is shown here hauling timbers to the New El Dorado Mill in 1913. Freight haulers often charged up to $20 per ton for materials hauled to remote mine sites. Getting water to the El Dorado was a constant challenge. Eventually, a pipeline was laid to Pinyon Well over nine miles west to bring water to the El Dorado Mill. The pipeline even included a public faucet for travelers.

Fred Vaile took this photograph of the directors of the New El Dorado Consolidated Mining Company in 1908. L.D. Johnson of Whittier, California, was president, and his son Charles, a mining engineer (shown in the rear wearing a cap), was named mine superintendent. Charles chose to focus development on Claim No. 14, the site of Chuckwalla Wilson's original discovery.

Fred Vaile, on horseback, succeeded Johnson as mine superintendent of the New El Dorado in 1912. He was able to maintain production at the mine throughout World War I, producing gold, galena, wulfenite, and molybdenite—all critical to wartime production. The New El Dorado claims were leased to John White of the White Mines Corporation during the 1920s.

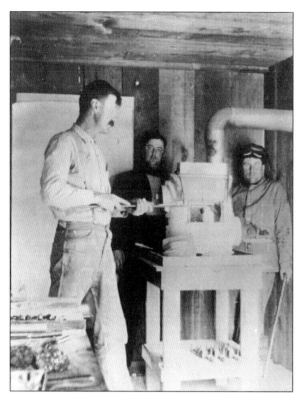

Mining at Gold Park dates to 1874, when the area was part of the Twentynine Palms mining district. As activity grew, Gold Park was organized as a separate district. The Gold Park Consolidated Mines Company held 52 claims in the area and developed a number of mines, including the Atlanta, Black Warrior, and the Gold Park Group. Shown here in the Gold Park assay office are, from left to right, C.W. Roach (manager), John Schweng (secretary), and W.E. Winnie (president). (Courtesy of the Twentynine Palms Historical Society.)

Miners at the Atlanta Mine drill an ore body sometime between 1905 and 1910. Mining was tough, physically demanding work under the best circumstances. As one miner put it, "It is such fearfully grueling labor—hacking away at solid rock in a tunnel . . . with practically no room to stand, no less to swing our picks . . . let it be said at this juncture that there is no more arduous labor than hard-rock mining."

Gold Park Consolidated built a central camp for its mining operations. The camp featured a bunkhouse, cookhouse, blacksmith shop, assay office, post office (briefly), and a private cabin for company officers. Up to 18 men were employed at Gold Park. Phil Sullivan worked on the Boss Mine and as a general caretaker and blacksmith. A Mrs. Ross was hired as a cook and used Joshua trees and yuccas for fuel. (Courtesy of the Twentynine Palms Historical Society.)

Mine workers at Gold Park No. 2 operate a one-stamp mill built to test ores. The mill was powered by a five-horsepower gas engine. Water in the tank above the mill was first hauled from Twentynine Palms, but this proved impractical for mine operations. Ivanpah Tank, near present-day Live Oak Picnic Area, was constructed in 1920, and water was piped nearly four miles to supply water for Gold Park mines.

The Gold Park area was operated, in part, with speculation in mind. Gold Park Consolidated had its main office in Los Angeles. Claims were often leased to other mining companies for further development. A visit to the Gold Park camp by John Schweng (middle) and W.E. Winnie (right), seated in a touring car behind chauffeur Johnson (?), was publicized by a Los Angeles newspaper with hopes of attracting additional investment in the area's mines. (Courtesy of the Twentynine Palms Historical Society.)

Though discovery and ownership of the Desert Queen Mine are shrouded in legend, the property was first developed by Bill McHaney with his brother Jim. In 1895, the first load of ore was hauled to Pinyon Well for milling and produced 97 ounces of gold from seven tons. Jim McHaney spent their new wealth freely, earning the name "Diamond Jim." Mired in unpaid bills and lawsuits over the mine, the McHaneys eventually lost the Desert Queen Mine and their longtime cattle ranch. The properties passed through several owners before being acquired by mining engineer William Morgan. Morgan hired Bill Keys as a caretaker and assayer at the Desert Queen. Though a solid producer of gold, the mine yielded only 23 ounces of gold and four ounces of silver in 1914, the year this photograph was taken. (Courtesy of the Twentynine Palms Historical Society.)

Since hauling ore from the Desert Queen to the distant Pinyon Well Mill was impractical, Jim McHaney had the Baker Iron Works construct a five-stamp mill at the Desert Queen Ranch. Baker ran the mill until it was paid off. The presence of water at the ranch and its proximity to the Desert Queen Mine made it an attractive mill site. The five-stamp mill remained at the ranch until 1948, when it was removed by Bill Keys. (Photograph by Ross Carmichael, courtesy of Frances Carmichael.)

Bill Keys acquired the Desert Queen Mine in 1918 from Morgan's estate for unpaid back wages. He remained owner of the Desert Queen Mine throughout his life, although he frequently leased it to others while charging them a $5 fee per ton to process the ore at his mills. Here, Keys hauls ore mined from the Desert Queen. Though modest in scale, Keys's mines were an important source of income for his family. (Courtesy of the Keys family.)

An arrastra was an early method for milling gold ore. The Pinto Wye Arrastra is one of the best preserved of its kind still found at its original location, although little is known of its origins. In an arrastra, a circular rock-lined pit serves as a channel for crushing the ore with heavy rocks attached to chains. The rocks are dragged around the pit using animal power or a gas engine. (Courtesy of the Library of Congress.)

Chester Pinkham's love of prospecting came from an early life spent in western mining camps with his father. Pinkham began prospecting in the Gold Park area around 1897. His search for mineral discoveries took him across Southern California, but he prospected most frequently in Riverside and San Bernardino Counties, where he filed more than 250 claims, including the Snow Cloud Mine. Pinkham Canyon is named for him. Here, Pinkham (left) is shown camping with John Thorsen.

As one of the few water sources on the Mecca-Dale freight route, Cottonwood Spring saw considerable traffic during the area's early mining history. Prospectors, freight haulers, and cattlemen all made use of the spring. Remains of a haul road from the 1880s can still be seen a quarter mile below the spring. By the 1890s, water was pumped from Cottonwood to the Iron Chief Mine. The spring produced 3,000 gallons of water a day in the early 1900s.

Matt Riley and a companion departed the Brooklyn Mine near Dale on July 4, 1905, for a trip to Mecca, some 60 miles away. Despite warnings, they left on foot with only a single canteen. They hoped to find water at Cottonwood Spring, 26 miles south. It was 104 degrees that day. When his companion turned back, Riley continued on alone. His dehydrated body was found less than a mile from the spring, and he was buried where he lay.

The Iron Chief Mine was actually a series of mines and almost 200 mineral claims stretched along approximately 10 miles of the eastern slopes of the Eagle Mountains. The Iron Chief Mine was operated by Charles Lane and later by William Stevens and Thomas Doffelmeyer. Ores of gold and copper assayed at $10 to $100 per ton, and from 1897 to 1902, the Iron Chief produced a $200,000 profit. But the Iron Chief's real wealth would prove to be its iron deposits. Mining engineer L.S. Barnes persuaded E.H. Harriman (pictured), president of the Southern Pacific Railroad, that he needed a western supply of iron to provide cheaper rails for the Southern Pacific. (Above, courtesy of the US Geological Survey; left, courtesy of the Library of Congress.)

Five

NEW PEOPLE, NEW WAYS
AN EVOLVING DESERT ETHIC

During the 1920s, Los Angeles grew to become America's fifth-largest city by the decade's close. By 1930, more than two million people lived in the Los Angeles region. America was becoming a car culture and a consumer society, and California was leading the way. With leisure time and the means of travel, urban Californians began to explore the desert regions of California for recreation.

Many who came to the desert, however, saw it as little more than a wasteland full of oddities. Much desert vegetation was dug up to decorate new urban homes or destroyed outright because people attached little value to the desert.

A few, however, began to see beauty and uniqueness in desert landscapes and sought to raise public awareness and appreciation for the desert. One of these was South Pasadena resident Minerva Hamilton Hoyt. Minerva Hamilton was born in Durant, Mississippi, and in 1897 came to Southern California with her husband, physician Albert Sherman Hoyt. In South Pasadena, she involved herself in many civic causes, but her greatest passion was for the desert and its preservation.

An avid gardener, Hoyt became fascinated by desert plants and began making weekend excursions to the desert. There, she saw how much wanton destruction was occurring, and she resolved to do something about it.

In the late 1920s, Hoyt prepared elaborate exhibits of desert plant life that were shown in New York, Boston, and at the Royal Horticultural Society Chelsea Flower Show in London, England. Her desert exhibits received public acclaim, and she developed a reputation as an advocate for the desert. She became the conservation chairwoman for the Garden Club in California, giving her a platform for her desert projects.

Her work came to the attention of noted landscape architect Frederick Law Olmsted Jr., who invited Hoyt to assist with the preparation of a California State Parks survey for the California governor and the State Parks Commission. Delivered in 1928, the report made recommendations for state parks and historic properties across California. Hoyt prepared the sections of the report dealing with the state's desert counties. Areas of high quality stands of Joshua trees were identified in the report, including the stands in the Little San Bernardino Mountains north of Palm Springs.

In 1930, she founded and became president of the International Desert Conservation League. One of the organization's goals was the establishment of a large desert park in Southern California, close to the region's growing population. Early efforts to interest the National Park Service (NPS) were not successful, as NPS director Horace Albright was focused on projects in Death Valley and the saguaro cactus desert of southern Arizona.

The 1932 election brought to Washington, DC, a Roosevelt administration looking to use the development and management of the national parks as a jobs creation program. However, before a federal park could be pursued, Hoyt had to fend off a bill passed by the California legislature that sought to create a state park in the Little San Bernardinos. It would have been smaller than her vision for a grand desert park and with little state land within its boundaries, Hoyt urged California governor James Rolph to veto the bill. The governor's veto of the state park bill coincided with a land transfer by the federal government to the state that eventually comprised the core of future Anza-Borrego Desert State Park.

Rolph also gave Hoyt a letter of introduction to President Roosevelt. Harold Ickes, interior secretary, became a supporter of the project, and he backed Hoyt's request to withdraw more than one million acres of public land to evaluate the area for designation as "Desert Plants National Park." This was accomplished by an executive order on October 25, 1933. Though significant problems existed with railroad lands, rights-of-way through the proposed south boundary, mining interests, and other private holdings, the creation of a desert park in the region became federal policy.

The NPS tasked Yellowstone superintendent Roger Toll with examining the area and reporting on its suitability as a new national park. Toll's visit to the area in March 1934 presented an unexpected obstacle for Hoyt. After a hurried tour to the area, Toll filed a 170-page report with a stunning conclusion: "It is believed that the area is not suitable for a national park." Toll instead recommended a 138,000-acre national monument focused on the granite formations and Joshua tree groves of the Lost Horse Valley area. The entire Colorado Desert region favored by Hoyt was omitted due to the interests of the mining industry and difficult land issues.

Hoyt was appalled and quickly organized a campaign to counter Toll's recommendations. Letters from Congress and the president of the US Chamber of Commerce were sent in support of her grand park concept. Eminent desert scientists Edmund Jaeger, Philip Munz, and Loye Miller also sent letters in support of the larger park.

To quell the controversy, NPS director Arno Cammerer tasked assistant director Harold C. Bryant with conducting a follow-up site inspection. Bryant, a scientist, educator, and California native quickly grasped the merits of the larger park Hoyt desired, but he warned her of the likely difficulties in getting the area established.

Hoyt traveled to Washington, DC, again in February 1935 and finally obtained a promise of support from the NPS to work on lands issues complicating her large park concept. Bryant himself took a leading role in negotiations with the Southern Pacific Company for either the purchase or exchange of railroad lands within the proposal.

After many difficult months of negotiations, it was clear that there was no way forward for a national monument that would encompass all of the 1,136,000 acres withdrawn under the 1933 executive order. Excluding many of the southern locations that Hoyt cherished, a national monument of 825,340 acres was delineated and received her reluctant support. On August 10, 1936, President Roosevelt, using authorities of the 1906 Antiquities Act, signed Proclamation 2193, establishing Joshua Tree National Monument, thus ending an epic struggle and forever cementing Minerva Hoyt's place in history as the "Apostle of the Cacti."

Beginning in the 1920s, the isolated valleys, scenic boulders, and iconic vegetation of the Little San Bernardino Mountains began to be valued for more than just their mineral wealth. However, it took a visionary South Pasadena resident, Minerva Hamilton Hoyt, to lead a campaign for a new national monument and a broader appreciation for the importance of deserts in their natural state.

Born on March 27, 1866, to a distinguished family of Mississippi landowners, young Minerva Hamilton attended finishing schools and music conservatories. She also learned about civic duty and politics from her father, Col. Joel George Hamilton, a Mississippi state senator and former Confederate regimental commander. From her mother, Emma Victoria Lockhart, she learned social graces and how to maneuver among the wealthy and the powerful. (Courtesy of the Minerva Hoyt family.)

Minerva Hamilton married Dr. Albert Sherman Hoyt and lived for a time in New York, Denver, and Baltimore. She and Hoyt had a son who died at a very young age. In 1897, they moved to South Pasadena, California, where she immersed herself in social activities such as gardening and supporting worthy causes. Sherman died in 1918, and his grieving wife devoted more time to social causes. (Courtesy of the Minerva Hoyt family.)

High society in Southern California offered many opportunities for an active life as a socialite and community leader. Minerva Hoyt served as president of the Los Angeles County Boys and Girls Aid Society. She was a leading member of the Valley Hunt Club that developed the Tournament of Roses Parade. She organized Red Cross blood drives in World War I and also was president of the Los Angeles Symphony Orchestra. (Courtesy of the Minerva Hoyt family.)

Gardening allowed her a way to pursue her interest in desert plant life. Her five-acre garden in South Pasadena was a community landmark. She began to take field trips to the desert, where she learned of the beauty and unique adaptations of desert plants. She also was appalled by the wanton destruction of desert plant life carried out by those who seemed to lack any feeling for the desert. (Courtesy of the Minerva Hoyt family.)

Minerva Hoyt resolved to educate people about the desert and developed desert plant exhibitions shown in New York, Boston, and the Royal Horticultural Society in London, England. Her garden exhibits recreated native desert landscapes and were very popular with the public. She would often have fresh desert plants flown to the exhibits so they would look as natural as possible. (Courtesy of the Minerva Hoyt family.)

Tapped to prepare a state parks survey for California, landscape architect Frederick Law Olmsted Jr. asked Minerva Hoyt to lend her expertise to the desert regions of the state. Olmsted's final report, submitted in December 1928, includes recommendations for parks in desert areas such as Death Valley, the Anza-Borrego Desert, and Red Rock Canyon. A park is also identified to preserve the outstanding population of Joshua trees.

Even as Olmsted issued his state parks report, desert areas identified for protection were under assault by plant collectors and vandals. The Devil's Garden area near Palm Springs was renowned for its cacti, but removal and destruction of mature plants in the area threatened its future preservation. Writing of the importance of the California desert, Olmsted notes in his report, "Nowhere else are casual thoughtless human changes in the landscape so irreparable." (Courtesy of the Palm Springs Art Museum, Stephen H. Willard Photography Collection & Archive.)

One especially tragic act of vandalism dramatically highlighted the need for desert protection. In the Antelope Valley, a giant Joshua tree more than 80 feet tall was set afire and destroyed on June 14, 1930. Minerva Hoyt and the league offered a $100 reward for the arrest of the perpetrator. In an article in the *South Pasadena Foothill Review*, she notes, "While the loss of this magnificent specimen is irreparable, the old giant will not have been sacrificed in vain if we can stimulate the public imagination to a definite program for the conservation of those remaining." (Right, photograph by Burton Frasher, courtesy of the NPS.)

Reward Offered For Slayer Of Giant Of Desert

Mrs. Sherman Hoyt, president of the International Desert Conservation League, has announced that a $100 reward will be paid by the league for the arrest and conviction of the persons, who wantonly burned the giant Joshua tree on the desert near Lancaster two weeks ago. Something of the enormous size of the tree is gained by the fact that the trunk was still burning when a photographer representing the league visited the scene, a week after it was set on fire.

THE
WESTERN
WOMAN

VOL. VI—NO. VI   December 1929 - January 1930   CONSERVATION NUMBER

MRS. A. SHERMAN HOYT
California Chairman Conservation - Garden Club of America
Founder and President—International Desert Conservation League

Her growing reputation and passion for desert preservation led Hoyt to found the International Desert Conservation League. Among its notable members were scientists such as botanist Philip Munz and ecologist Edmund Jaeger, educators, and several noted government officials, including Gifford Pinchot of the US Forest Service and Horace Albright, the NPS director. The league focused on establishing protected areas as one its primary goals.

Minerva Hoyt wrote to Horace Albright in 1930, seeking support for creating a national park in the desert mountains northeast of Palm Springs. Her vision for a one-million-acre park would take in outstanding examples of the Mojave and Colorado Desert ecosystems as well as extensive Joshua tree stands and scenic desert landforms. However, Albright was not supportive, as the service was committed to park projects at Death Valley and the saguaro cactus forest near Tucson, Arizona. (Courtesy of the Library of Congress.)

In 1931, Hoyt and the International Desert Conservation League were invited to survey the deserts of Mexico and make recommendations to the government on sites for desert parks and reserves. The group journeyed through the Sonoran Desert in western Mexico, toured cactus deserts in the Guadalajara area, and visited columnar cactus forests near Tehuacán in Puebla and at Teotitlán in Oaxaca. Prof. Ramirez Laguna, chief botanist at the National University, accompanied the group. (Courtesy of the Minerva Hoyt family.)

In Mexico City, Hoyt met with Mexican president Pascual Ortiz Rubio (right) at Chapultepec Castle. President Rubio promised to set aside a 10,000-acre reserve in the cactus forests of Tehuacán as a monument to the conservation work of Hoyt and the league. A species of Mexican cactus was named in her honor, and President Rubio dubbed her "the Apostle of the Cacti." The man at left is unidentified. (Courtesy of the Minerva Hoyt family.)

California governor James Rolph introduced Hoyt to Pres. Franklin D. Roosevelt (left). Shown here visiting Yellowstone National Park with Yellowstone superintendent Edmund Rogers and First Lady Eleanor Roosevelt, Roosevelt saw development of parks as a way to build jobs and local economies during the Great Depression. Roosevelt's executive order in 1933 withdrew 1,136,000 acres of public land for study as a proposed Desert Plants National Park. (Courtesy of the Library of Congress.)

Secretary of the Interior Harold Ickes carried out New Deal–era public lands policy for the Roosevelt administration. Ickes met with Minerva Hoyt in the summer of 1933 and provided crucial support for her desert park proposal. He told Hoyt, "The President is for it, and I am for it." (Courtesy of the Library of Congress.)

Roger Wolcott Toll was superintendent of Yellowstone National Park from 1929 until his untimely death in an automobile accident in 1936. He was responsible for evaluating new park proposals for the NPS and conducted a California Desert inspection trip in March 1934. Toll felt the desert plants park proposal had issues with land acquisition, management challenges, and, in his view, a lack of nationally significant features.

Dr. Philip A. Munz was a professor of botany at Pomona College and a widely published expert on California desert flora. Dr. Munz was part of the 1931 Mexico survey party and accompanied Minerva Hoyt on Toll's NPS inspection tour in March 1934. As an honorary vice president of the International Desert Conservation League, Munz was a tireless supporter of a large desert park to encompass outstanding tracts of both the Colorado and Mojave Deserts.

Minerva Hoyt's concept for Desert Plants National Park featured not only expanses of Joshua trees, but also many Colorado Desert localities such as Hidden Springs Canyon, Corn Springs, and the Salton Sea. Land ownership conflicts with the railroads, state lands, and private holdings would pose major obstacles for inclusion of these areas. Hidden Spring Canyon, shown here, included a native palm oasis and deeply eroded sedimentary rock formations.

In his report, Toll recommended a much smaller national monument containing the Joshua tree forests and granite boulder formations of the Lost Horse Valley, Hidden Valley (shown here), and Queen Valley areas. He was concerned with complex lands issues, Metropolitan Water District rights, and the opinion of the mining industry that the area should remain open to mining. Toll's findings were bitterly opposed by Hoyt and her Conservation League supporters.

NPS director Arno Cammerer had to navigate cautiously between Minerva Hoyt and her park boosters; his own supervisor, Harold Ickes, who also backed a desert park; and the opinions of senior park officials Roger Toll and Conrad Wirth, who saw difficulties with the Hoyt proposal. Cammerer chose to get a second opinion and directed Harold Bryant to conduct a second inspection tour.

Protest over Toll's report from park backers included letters from most of the California congressional delegation and other prominent scientists and business executives. In response, the NPS decided on another inspection, only this time it sent assistant director Harold Bryant, a biologist and native Californian. Bryant recognized the ecological significance of the larger park, but he warned Hoyt of the difficulties posed by the Colorado River Aqueduct and other private lands within her park proposal. (Courtesy of Grand Canyon National Park.)

The Colorado River Aqueduct, owned by the metropolitan water district, was constructed during the 1930s, even as Minerva Hoyt pressed for a national park in the area. Pumping stations lifted water hundreds of feet over the Coxcomb and Eagle Mountains (shown here), bringing water to Los Angeles. The presence of a major industrial project along the park's southern boundary was of great concern to Toll and other NPS officials. (Courtesy of the Library of Congress.)

In 1932, Congress gave the Metropolitan Water District a 250-foot right-of-way for its aqueduct, and development included roads, power lines, pumping stations, tunnels, and workers' camps. It was a massive industrial project for a proposed national park. Despite the obvious conflict, general counsel James H. Howard backed the Hoyt park proposal saying, "I am told these . . . areas support many rare desert plants which should be preserved." (Courtesy of the Library of Congress.)

Park Service inspector P.T. Primm investigated land use conflicts along the proposed park's southern boundary. During a May 1935 visit, Primm found water district activities had damaged vegetation in some areas. However, he also found the NPS was unable to prevent such work due to preexisting rights held by the water district. Here, Primm examines a handsome Joshua tree during his inspection trip.

The Southern Pacific Railroad owned thousands of acres of land within the proposed park. Hoyt sought the help of Susan Delano McKelvey, a noted Southwestern botanist and a cousin of President Roosevelt. McKelvey contacted Henry de Forest, a board member for Southern Pacific, asking him to persuade the railroad to sell or donate its inholdings. This effort was ultimately unsuccessful, leading Hoyt to reluctantly accept smaller national monument boundaries with assurances from the Park Service that future efforts would be made to acquire the excluded lands. (Courtesy of the Arnold Arboretum Horticultural Library, Harvard University.)

Beginning in the 1920s, Minerva Hoyt would dedicate much of her life to educating people about the beauty of the desert and leading efforts to protect it. Hoyt realized her dream when, on August 10, 1936, Pres. Franklin D. Roosevelt signed a presidential proclamation designating the 825,340-acre Joshua Tree National Monument. (Courtesy of the Palm Springs Art Museum, Stephen H. Willard Photography Collection & Archive.)

Six

GROWING PAINS
A NEW NATIONAL MOVEMENT

The early years of Joshua Tree National Monument were tumultuous, as the new NPS unit faced a host of problems and external pressures. Initially placed under the supervision of Yosemite National Park, Joshua Tree received numerous visits and inspection trips by senior park officials as the future of the new monument was debated and planned. Supt. Charles G. Thomson of Yosemite appointed Yosemite park naturalist James Cole as the on-site custodian at Joshua Tree.

From the outset, there was intense opposition to the new monument from mining interests. While existing claims within Joshua Tree could still be worked, no new mining claims were allowed within monument boundaries. Congress had permitted the filing of new claims in Death Valley National Monument, and many argued the same should be done at Joshua Tree. Over the objections of the NPS, Congressman Harry Sheppard several times introduced legislation to open Joshua Tree to mining. The mining controversy led to an internal debate with the NPS over whether significant portions of the eastern part of the monument should be eliminated from the new unit. The area's remoteness, complex land ownership, and perceived lack of recreation potential led some park officials to recommend its eventual removal from the monument as a way to resolve the mining question.

While the mining and lands issues were debated, James Cole worked to get Joshua Tree up and running. An office was opened in Twentynine Palms in September 1940. The first field positions were hired in 1941, including ranger Harold Hildreth and Robert Lake as grader-vehicle operator. Several congressmen paid visits, and the first public use numbers showed 23,964 people visited Joshua Tree National Monument in 1941.

The attack on Pearl Harbor and the United States' entry into World War II had an enormous effect on the area. As the United States ramped up its war effort, national parks were called on to play their part. Gen. George S. Patton established the Desert Training Center to prepare troops for mechanized warfare under harsh field conditions. Field camps were created at numerous desert locations, including Camp Young and Camp Coxcomb, which bordered the monument. James Cole and other park staff entered military service, resulting in many short-term assignments to Joshua Tree by temporary replacements.

The war also had a significant effect on mining and ranching activity. During the 1930s, mining activity increased as the Depression and higher gold prices lured many unemployed workers into mining. Mines at Dale and Gold Park expanded operations, while new prospects such as the Golden Bee, the Blue Bell, and the Mastodon were located and developed. In 1942, the War Production Board shut down gold mining in the United States except for essential production, so many mines in the Joshua Tree area ceased operation. One exception was iron. In 1944, the Henry J. Kaiser Corporation bought the Eagle Mountain iron claims from the Southern Pacific Railroad, and large-scale iron mining began at the site.

Many national parks were opened to grazing operations during the war. The NPS determined that one grazing permit could be issued at Joshua Tree, and James Stocker, a San Bernardino County sheriff, and Bill Keys applied to receive the permit.

Efforts to expand his livestock operation ultimately led Bill Keys into a fateful confrontation with Worth Bagley, a retired Los Angeles County sheriff who had settled on a homestead near

Wall Street Mill. Animosity over property rights and trespass issues built up between them until on May 11, 1943, Bagley accosted Keys. Bagley fired a single errant shot as Keys was returning home after watering his cattle in Queen Valley. Keys returned fire, killing Bagley in self-defense. He was tried and convicted of manslaughter and sentenced to San Quentin Prison. With Keys's conviction, the NPS awarded the wartime grazing permit to Stocker, another blow to Keys's family.

Keys served five years before he was paroled. At the request of Frances Keys, author Erle Stanley Gardner and his Court of Last Resort looked into the Keys case. With the help of state assemblyman Vernon Kilpatrick and statements from Bagley's widow, Isabelle Clark, Gov. Goodwin Knight gave Keys a full pardon on July 24, 1956.

Following World War II, Joshua Tree's mining controversy was rekindled. The wartime prohibition on gold mining was repealed in 1946, and Congressman Harry Sheppard again introduced bills to reduce the size of Joshua Tree to allow mining. Ironically, his bills were opposed not only by the monument's supporters, but also by miners who wanted the entire area open to mining. With the death of Minerva Hoyt in 1945, Joshua Tree lost its most ardent champion. While Sheppard would fail in his efforts to redraw monument boundaries, Congressman John Phillips, whose district included much of the monument, would ultimately succeed. In September 1950, Phillips's bill became Public Law 81-837 and removed 289,500 acres from Joshua Tree National Monument, one of the largest acreage reductions of any NPS unit.

With the boundary reduction decided, the NPS was now able to focus on developing visitor facilities and creating programs to manage the site's vast natural and cultural resources. After years of negotiation, the NPS accepted a donation of 58 acres of land on January 10, 1950, from the Twentynine Palms Corporation, allowing the monument to establish its official headquarters at the historic Oasis of Mara in Twentynine Palms. From 1950 to 1954, workers built walkways, a retaining wall, an office building, and a small museum exhibit. A dedication ceremony was held on April 7, 1954.

Superintendent Cole identified 118 miles of roads that were graded and incorporated into the monument's 1941 master plan. These roads still form the core of today's park road system. A new controversy emerged over the construction of a north-south road through the rugged Little San Bernardino Mountains. Riverside County wanted to provide a more direct route across the monument for growing Coachella Valley communities. This idea was strongly opposed by the NPS, yet the idea continued to be advocated by local interests throughout the 1950s.

The first visitor camping facilities were constructed in the spring of 1950 at Jumbo Rocks, Hidden Valley, Indian Cove, and Cottonwood Spring. White Tank Campground was opened a year later. By 1953, interpretive trails at the Oasis of Mara, the Cholla Cactus Garden, Arch Rock, and Cap Rock were completed and opened for public use. A year later, the Indian Cove Nature Trail was added, and new entrance signs featuring the NPS arrowhead symbol were erected. By the mid-1950s, visitation at the monument topped 300,000 people, and Joshua Tree finally began to live up to its promise as a tourist destination.

Spearheaded by NPS director Conrad Wirth, the Mission 66 program brought some of the first significant federal funds for park development to Joshua Tree. Planners designed modern visitor facilities to serve a recreation-oriented postwar population. The program led to the construction of the Oasis Visitor Center, campgrounds, trails, and picnic areas.

While the 1960s marked the beginning of Joshua Tree's modern era, it also spelled the end of its frontier period. Frances's death in 1963 led Bill Keys to sell the ranch a year later to businessman Henry Tubman, although Keys was allowed to live out his life at the ranch. In 1966, the monument acquired Keys Ranch in a land exchange with Tubman. Following Keys's death, it faced a decision on how to manage the site. A debate ensued over whether the ranch should be carefully preserved or allowed to weather and decay naturally. When the ranch was added to the National Register of Historic Places and highlighted during the 1976 bicentennial, preservation won out. Rangers now conduct guided tours of the ranch for the public. A handful of active mining claims and various holdings still existed in the monument, but Joshua Tree's future would now revolve around new environmental laws, external boundary issues, and growing public use.

Charles Thomson, superintendent at Yosemite, took charge of the new national monument. He made his first visit to the area in October 1936 and was surprised by the landscape and rich flora of the new site. However, he was concerned by its lack of water. Though Thomson died in 1937, he recommended that visitor facilities be minimized due to the water situation and the presence of nearby communities.

Thomson appointed Yosemite naturalist James Cole as custodian of the new park. Cole was not given the title of superintendent until 1940. With limited NPS experience, Cole carried out his new duties with little budget or staff, facing complex mining and land issues all while fending off personal attacks from Bill Keys and others over his management of the monument. Cole's tenure was interrupted by wartime service. He transferred to the agency's Omaha, Nebraska, office in 1947.

In the mid-1930s, Euloge "Frenchy" Auclair worked several claims near the El Dorado called the Golden Bee Mine. A colorful character, Auclair arrived in the area with no prior mining experience, but he was nonetheless able to locate and work a successful gold mine. Ore was processed at the Gold Crown Mill and other custom mills, yielding $50 a ton in gold. Auclair's wife, Marie, and their two children lived at the rugged and remote site. (Courtesy of the Twentynine Palms Historical Society.)

Several claims just north of the El Dorado made up the Blue Bell Mine. In 1936, Matt Rogers of Twentynine Palms hired Bob Saunders and Dave Carroll as laborers and partners to work one level of the Blue Bell. In return for their labor, Saunders and Carroll shared in the profits from the mine. Here, Saunders operates a hoist powered by an automobile engine at the Blue Bell. (Courtesy of the Twentynine Palms Historical Society.)

Bill Keys owned the Desert Queen Mine, but he often leased the site to others who did the actual mining. Keys made money by processing ore from the Desert Queen, either at the mill located at his ranch or the Wall Street Mill. During the 1930s, a succession of people tried their hand at mining the Desert Queen, but by 1941, production had essentially stopped.

In 1929, Oran Booth and several partners located the Wall Street millsite. Bill Keys acquired the site in 1930 and sold it with the Gold Tiger Mine and the two-stamp mill at Pinyon Well to a family named Oberer. The Oberers moved the stamp mill from Pinyon Well to the Wall Street site, but before long they defaulted on the property. Keys reacquired it, rebuilt the stamp mill, and began milling gold at the Wall Street Mill. (Photograph by Ross Carmichael, courtesy of Frances Carmichael.)

The Phelps family—Charles, Della, and their daughter Merla—leased several Joshua Tree mines in the 1930s, including the Lost Horse and Desert Queen. The Phelpses began working the Desert Queen in 1935. They installed a cyanide processing operation that allowed for the treatment of older mine tailings. A ball mill crushed ore fine enough for cyanide processing. By 1938, the Phelpses left the desert having produced only about 40 ounces of gold at the Desert Queen. (Courtesy of the Twentynine Palms Historical Society.)

George Hulsey of Indio located claims near Cottonwood Spring for the Mastodon Mine and Winona Mill. The mine operated from 1934 to 1939. The millsite used a ball mill for crushing, and ore was treated through amalgamation and cyanide processes. One assay from the Mastodon claim returned a value of $744 per ton. The Hulseys lived in a cabin on the property and continued the assessment work until 1971.

Bill McHaney

As he grew older, Bill McHaney would occasionally leave his miner's shack in Music Valley to stay during the winter with the Keys family. In 1933, he filed on a 160-acre homestead near the entrance to Barker Dam and lived there for a time. As his health declined, he eventually moved to Keys Ranch in a small cabin of his own. He died on January 5, 1937. (Photograph by Burton Frasher, courtesy of the NPS.)

Jim Stocker was a San Bernardino County deputy sheriff who also had cattle ranching interests in the area. Stocker bought the cattle holdings of Katherine Barry in 1936. During World War II, he also acquired Warren's Well. Grazing in national parks was encouraged during the war, and Stocker competed with Bill Keys for the single grazing permit that was issued. Stocker received the permit when Keys was sent to prison in 1943. (Courtesy of the Twentynine Palms Historical Society.)

In January 1941, Harold Hildreth was hired as the first park ranger at Joshua Tree. He was replaced by clerk-ranger John Stratton (pictured), who arrived in October 1941 from Lassen Volcanic National Park. Stratton soon left for wartime service in the Army. He returned in 1946, was promoted to park ranger, and enjoyed a long NPS career serving as superintendent at several other parks. After retirement, Stratton returned to Twentynine Palms and became a board member for the Joshua Tree Natural History Association and a local church member.

Early park managers thought that wildfires were unlikely in the desert due to its sparse vegetation. Tragically, on July 4, 1942, they were proven wrong. A fire started on the Randolph inholding in Lost Horse Valley and quickly burned onto monument lands. The small park staff mobilized to fight the fire, and Pete Mahrt, a roads foreman, was killed by smoke inhalation, becoming the first park employee to die while on duty.

With the December 1941 attack on Pearl Harbor, the United States found itself in a worldwide conflict. Gen. George S. Patton needed to train tank and ground troops under realistic battlefield conditions to fight the German Afrika Corps in the North African desert. He established numerous bases, mainly in California and Arizona. Camp Young, shown here in May 1942, was located just south of the monument near Cottonwood Spring and served as headquarters for Patton's training program. (Courtesy of the General Patton Museum.)

In this US Signal Corps photograph, an M5 tank maneuvers through granite boulders and Colorado Desert vegetation near the southern boundary of Joshua Tree National Monument in August 1942. Despite pressure to open national parks for military use, NPS officials opposed the use of tanks and other military equipment in the new monument. In 1943, it was discovered that Army troops has graded a road in the Pinto Basin for military use. Duane Jacobs, appointed interim superintendent while James Cole was on active duty, tried to persuade military commanders to repair the damage. (Courtesy of the General Patton Museum.)

Bill Keys (left) and his neighbor Worth Bagley often argued over property and cattle trespass issues. Their enmity turned deadly in May 1943 when Bagley confronted Keys near their property boundary and fired at him. Keys returned fire, mortally wounding Bagley. Though he claimed self-defense, Keys was convicted and sent to prison. Frances Keys asked author/attorney Erle Stanley Gardner to look into Bill's case. Gardner and his colleagues with the Court of Last Resort—volunteer legal experts who examined cases of questionable justice—helped secure parole for Keys in 1948 and eventually a pardon from the governor. At home after his release, Keys shows ore samples to Raymond Schindler (right) of the Court of Last Resort. (Left, Ross Carmichael photograph, courtesy of Frances Carmichael.)

Bill Keys called the time in prison his "college years," as he read and took up calligraphy and painting. He tried to resume his former life after his pardon, working gypsum claims in the Palen Mountains and improving dams at the Ranch and Barker Dam, but the family faced financial hardship from his legal troubles. To mark his fateful encounter with Bagley, Keys carved an inscription into a granite marker and mounted it at the site of the shoot-out.

Following the war, Kaiser expanded its Eagle Mountain mining operation. A rail line was built in 1947 to connect with the main Southern Pacific line near the Salton Sea. A Kaiser steel mill built at Fontana, California, relied heavily on Eagle Mountain iron. The town of Eagle Mountain grew on the site, and Kaiser's efforts to obtain water from wells on monument land in the lower Pinto Basin led to growing conflicts with the NPS. (Courtesy of the Bureau of Mines.)

The battle over mining at Joshua Tree led to the formation of a new conservation organization focused on deserts. In 1954, Randall Henderson of *Desert Magazine*, ecologist Edmund Jaeger, and numerous others formed the Desert Protective Council to help protect Joshua Tree from mining. Shown here at Indian Cove Campground, members of the Desert Protective Council gather to socialize and discuss strategy in October 1956. Jaeger is seated at left.

As early as 1937, California congressman Harry Sheppard introduced legislation into the House of Representatives to open all of Joshua Tree National Monument to new mining claims. He later changed his position to advocate eliminating large areas of the monument from National Park Service control. After years of public debate and controversy, it was a bill by Congressman John Phillips that in 1950 reduced Joshua Tree by 289,000 acres, removing much of the Colorado Desert landscape Minerva Hoyt fought to preserve. (Courtesy of the Library of Congress.)

Frank Givens replaced James Cole as superintendent of Joshua Tree in 1947. In addition to the mining controversy, land acquisition and development of visitor facilities would be his top priorities at the site. One success came when the Twentynine Palms Corporation donated 58 acres at the east end of the Oasis of Mara for use as a park headquarters. The historic and ecological value of the oasis, plus access to water, made it an ideal location.

Park officials worried about the presence of so much nonfederal land within Joshua Tree's boundaries. In 1945, developer Dick Curtis announced plans to purchase nearly 3,500 acres of Southern Pacific Railroad land in Lost Horse Valley (shown above) for a Western film set and town called Pioneertown. The location was in the heart of the park's primary scenic area and would permanently alter the character of the monument. Superintendents Cole and Givens and NPS realty specialists negotiated a complicated land swap and purchase, with Curtis acquiring public land northwest of Yucca Valley and the monument receiving more than 12,800 acres of railroad lands in Lost Horse Valley. Pioneertown was built by Curtis with Western film stars Roy Rogers and Dale Evans. Here, they are shown riding in a 1947 parade held to celebrate the new "Old West" town. Pictured are Rogers (left, holding unidentified child), Curtis, and Evans. (Below, courtesy of the Morongo Basin Historical Society.)

While the study of natural resources received scant attention relative to mining and lands issues, some initial surveys of the flora and fauna were carried out. Alden Miller (left), shown here with Jim Cole and youngster Hugh Zimmer, carried out early bird and mammal surveys in the 1940s. Miller later coauthored *The Lives of Desert Animals at Joshua Tree National Monument* with Robert C. Stebbins. (Photograph by Harlow Jones, courtesy of the NPS.)

Park service biologist Lowell Sumner, seen here in 1950, made early studies of park wildlife, looking specifically at the effects that mining and the proposed boundary reductions would have on native animals. Sumner, along with Cole and Lawrence Merriam, argued for the NPS to keep the Pinto Basin and seek to extend the monument boundary to the Colorado River Aqueduct to protect bighorn sheep. They were among the few service employees advocating retention of the original monument boundaries.

Early park planners suggested that park roads be maintained as unpaved but graded for safety. A 25-miles-per-hour speed limit was thought sufficient for visitor travel. Development of a better road to Keys View was an early priority. The great number of inholdings made road improvements difficult in some locations. The monument's first paved road, from Twentynine Palms to Keys View, was dedicated in 1950. Better roads helped boost visitation to 141,416 in 1952, a nearly twentyfold jump from 1944.

In 1951, viewing scopes were installed at Keys View, one of the park's early interpretive services. The overlook is a popular visitor attraction, with dramatic views of the Coachella Valley and surrounding mountains. Bill Keys built the first road to the site in 1926. NPS officials changed the overlook's name to Salton View in the 1940s, arguing that federal policy precluded naming features for living persons. Years later, it was changed back to Keys View.

With the acquisition of the Oasis of Mara property, work began on construction of the park's official headquarters. An administrative office, covered patios, public restrooms, and a small exhibit were built. On April 3, 1954, a dedication ceremony for the new headquarters complex was held, and over 500 people attended. Here, Supt. Samuel King addresses the assembled audience during the ceremony.

Though several camping areas had been set aside by 1949, campground development began in earnest in 1950 with fireplaces, pit toilets, and tables installed at Cottonwood Springs, Jumbo Rocks, Hidden Valley, and Indian Cove. By 1954, nine park campgrounds had been established. Visitation topped 320,000 in 1960 as visitor facilities throughout the monument improved.

Recreational use of horses in the monument also received attention from park managers in the plans for new visitor facilities. Here, a group of riders takes a test ride in 1956 on a proposed trail. Ryan Campground was also planned and built with equestrian users in mind.

Rod Smith and his father, Phil Smith, were pioneer rock climbers at Joshua Tree. Phil was a National Park Service employee who worked at Grand Teton National Park as well as Joshua Tree. They were active rock climbers and achieved a number of first ascents at the monument during a time when few others climbed. Rod took this dramatic photograph of his father Phil making the first ascent of Saddle Rock in 1956. (Courtesy of Rod Smith.)

Like all national parks, natural features are protected at Joshua Tree. The protection and preservation of native desert plant life was a primary reason behind Minerva Hoyt's park advocacy. Yet even with the establishment of the national monument, plant collection and poaching continued. Here, a Joshua Tree ranger examines illegally collected plants confiscated from park visitors during a weeklong traffic study in 1958.

The Mission 66 program was intended to provide the nation with a major upgrade to park visitor facilities to coincide with the agency's 50th anniversary in 1966. Visitor center construction was a hallmark of the program, and Joshua Tree saw its new facility built at the Oasis of Mara between 1961 and 1964. The project featured exhibits, a book sales area, picnic tables, and staff offices, giving visitors a greatly improved educational experience during their park visit.

Seven

WILDERNESS PARK IN AN URBAN LANDSCAPE
THE ENVIRONMENTAL ERA

Bill Keys died on June 29, 1969, leaving behind a property that would form a cornerstone of Joshua Tree's history. His passing turned the monument's focus toward a host of issues centered around the passage of new environmental laws in the 1960s and early 1970s. New legal requirements addressing historic preservation, environmental protection, endangered species, and preservation of wilderness strengthened park protection but required special knowledge and skills within the park staff.

The 1964 Wilderness Act directed federal agencies to identify government land having potential as wilderness—lands forever protected from development—under the terms of the law. Joshua Tree carried out the mandated studies and sought input on its wilderness recommendations to Congress. Public sentiment, expressed through official comments and testimony at hearings, generally favored more wilderness than the monument first proposed. On October 20, 1976, Pres. Gerald R. Ford signed Public Law 94-567, establishing 429,690 acres of the monument as wilderness, more than three-fourths of its total lands.

Under the Mission 66 program, the monument addressed its needs for improved visitor facilities as visitation continued to grow, reaching 643,000 in 1970. The Cottonwood area received considerable attention in the mid-1960s, as a new campground was built away from the ecologically sensitive Cottonwood Spring, and a visitor contact station and employee residences were added to handle visitors entering Joshua Tree from the south. In 1970, a ranger station and residence were built at Indian Cove.

Faced with increased legal requirements for resource protection and a need for professional expertise, Supt. Rick Anderson appointed Robert Moon, an ecologist, to head Joshua Tree's first formal resource management program in 1981. Among the monument's important resource issues were the spread of exotic plants, removal of feral burros, management of endangered species such as the desert tortoise, establishing a program to monitor growing air pollution, abandoned mine safety, and understanding the effects of larger and more frequent wildfires at Joshua Tree National Park.

The growth of park visitation to over 1,000,000 by 1990 meant the small protection ranger staff was faced with an increasing number of complex search-and-rescue operations. When 3-year-old Laura Bradbury went missing from Indian Cove Campground in October 1984, Joshua Tree found itself managing a complex search that became a national news story and a family tragedy as the toddler was never found. Joshua Tree Search and Rescue (JOSAR), a team of park staff and volunteers, was formed in 1982 to improve park search and climbing rescue capabilities.

The 1976 Federal Lands Policy Act directed the Bureau of Land Management to develop a conservation plan for the entire 25,000,000-acre California desert. The plan included an inventory of wilderness lands as well as areas identified for special management as environmentally sensitive, scenic, or recreation areas. Calls began to be heard for creation of a new national park in the

East Mojave as well as expansion of Death Valley and Joshua Tree National Monuments and designating them as national parks.

A long and sometimes rancorous public debate ensued over the future of the California desert with off-road vehicle, sportsmen, and some business groups opposed to increased protection for the desert and environmental organizations enthusiastically supportive.

Eventually, conservationists urged that Congress pass a bill to decide the desert's future. Sen. Alan Cranston introduced the first version of the California Desert Protection Act in 1986. However, it was not until new California senator Dianne Feinstein and Congressman Rick Lehman introduced revised bills in 1993 that the legislation began to move forward. With support of the newly elected Clinton administration, the act was passed and signed into law on October 31, 1994. The landmark legislation created a new Mojave National Preserve, added well over a million acres to the new Death Valley National Park, and increased Joshua Tree National Monument by 234,000 acres, also giving it national park status. Minerva Hoyt's wish for a national park was finally granted nearly 60 years later.

Supt. Ernest Quintana and his staff had little time to celebrate, as a new and serious threat to the new national park began to emerge. The Mine Reclamation Corporation, a subsidiary of Kaiser Ventures, proposed to use the inactive Eagle Mountain Mine as the site for a solid-waste landfill. At peak operation, the new garbage dump would receive as much as 20,000 tons of waste a day and operate for over 100 years. It would be the world's largest landfill, located just three-fourths of a mile from the park's southeast boundary.

First proposed in 1988, the Eagle Mountain Landfill underwent an extensive environmental review. The park and many environmental organizations expressed alarm over the effects the landfill would have on air quality, on wildlife around the landfill, and on the park's wilderness values, including its pristine night skies. Equally troubling was the uncertain damage to the park's visitation and its public image if it became known as the "dump park."

When senior NPS officials in Washington, DC, favored an agreement with the corporation to provide funding to study the landfill's effects, it was left to the environmental community to mount opposition to the giant landfill. Two unlikely figures emerged to lead that battle. Donna and Larry Charpied, local jojoba farmers who lived near the proposed project, became highly effective spokespersons opposing the massive dump. The Charpieds and their allies faced years of legal battles, with many defeats and victories along the way as the project and its environmental studies were challenged and debated in state, then federal courts. Federal court rulings against the landfill occurred in 2005 and 2009, and the project appeared defeated when the US Supreme Court refused to hear the case in 2011. Mine Reclamation Corporation filed for bankruptcy.

While dealing with Eagle Mountain and other external threats, the park issued its general management plan in 1996. The plan led to development of a wilderness and backcountry management plan in 2000 that formalized a 270-mile trail system for the park and defined park policies on equestrian and wilderness use. Management of rock climbing was a major focus of the wilderness plan as the park became concerned with impacts of the sport's rapid growth at Joshua Tree.

In the late 1990s, financial support from the Federal Lands Highway Program and funds generated from visitor fees allowed the park to upgrade its aging and often inadequate infrastructure. By 1998, park visitation topped 1.4 million people, and improvements were clearly needed. Roads, campgrounds, picnic areas, visitor centers, entrance stations, and trails all received funds, and many new projects were carried out.

The year 2011 marked the 75th anniversary of Joshua Tree National Monument (now National Park). A yearlong celebration was planned and carried out with many special events, new partnerships, and reflection on the park's past and its future. Development projects along park boundaries still cropped up like exotic weeds, and the new threat of climate change loomed ominously. Yet the park had many friends on hand ready to defend its worth and integrity. Much has changed, but Minerva Hoyt's determined advocacy remains alive among the park's Joshua trees.

In the last years of his life, Bill Keys continued making improvements to the ranch (see the scaffolding in the background). He envisioned the ranch as a resort and worked on his dams in hopes of creating a fishery for tourists. He even had a brief acting career, appearing in two Disney films created for its television programs. A large crowd of more than 100 people braved the summer heat to attend Keys's funeral in July 1969.

Located seven miles north of Interstate 10, Cottonwood Visitor Center provided a convenient information stop for visitors entering the park from the south. Shown here in 1968, the contact station soon proved far too small to serve the area's visitors. By 1995, annual traffic exceeded 104,000 people, and crowds commonly backed up into the parking lot. It was replaced in 1997 with a larger modular building.

An important addition to the monument's visitor facilities was the acquisition in 1976 of the private Jellystone Park Campground at Black Rock. Equipped with a swimming pool, tennis court, and an array of statuary based on Hanna-Barbera's popular Yogi Bear cartoon, Jellystone gave the park a new campground, visitor center, and staging area for equestrian riders. In 2000, an interagency fire center shared with the Bureau of Land Management was built on the 80-acre site.

During Homer Rouse's tenure as superintendent at Joshua Tree from 1973 to 1976, a master plan draft and wilderness recommendations were prepared. Rouse, like many superintendents, took a conservative approach to wilderness planning. Though providing the greatest measure of land protection, wilderness also removed much of the flexibility park managers were accustomed to exercising in preparing their long-range plans. The final wilderness bill established 429,690 acres of wilderness at Joshua Tree, over 100,000 acres more than the service's first recommendations.

As Joshua Tree faced more threats from external development, park managers recognized that wilderness designation offered many advantages in helping the agency meet its preservation mission. The California Desert Protection Act and later legislation designated even more of Joshua Tree's lands as wilderness, bringing its total wilderness acreage to 594,502. Another 70,600 acres are classed as potential wilderness. The remote and rugged Coxcomb Mountains are included within the Joshua Tree Wilderness.

Joshua Tree's granite boulders attract rock climbers from all over the world. Inevitably, accidents occur, and climbers sustain serious injuries or fatalities in falls. Rangers and search-and-rescue volunteers train constantly to sharpen their skills and techniques. Here, rangers practice lowering a litter during a 1970s training exercise. In 1982, Joshua Tree Search and Rescue was formed to build and improve on the park's search-and-rescue capabilities.

As late as 1964, women were barred from applying for many ranger positions, and they were not allowed to wear the same uniform as male rangers until 1978. Susan Luckie Reilly was a ranger-naturalist at Joshua Tree in the 1960s and often gave programs about the park to local children. Here, she wears the "stewardess" uniform designed specifically for female rangers. Reilly's father, Dr. James Luckie, is regarded as the founder of the town of Twentynine Palms.

Supt. Rick Anderson hired Robert "Bob" Moon in 1981 to become the park's first chief of resources. An ecologist, Moon brought expertise that had been missing from Joshua Tree's natural and cultural resource program. One issue Moon and his fledgling staff faced was that of exotic animals, including goldfish released by visitors at Barker Dam. As the water evaporated, periodic goldfish "roundups" were held, and the unwelcome fish were given away.

Studies showed that access to water was a chief factor limiting bighorn sheep populations at Joshua Tree. Prominent biologists recommended installing artificial water sources called guzzlers in the Joshua Tree backcountry to aid bighorn survival. Numerous guzzlers were built in the monument, but they were difficult to operate and maintain. The use of guzzlers has been a difficult issue for park managers, as the devices appear to conflict with wilderness law and NPS policies favoring natural management.

Control of exotic species at Joshua Tree included a small population of feral burros discovered roaming the monument in the early 1980s. With public sentiment strongly opposed to shooting burros, the monument staff organized a live capture program in the Pushawalla Canyon area. In August 1985, four burro wranglers try to coax several animals into a corral. Captured burros were turned over to the Bureau of Land Management's Adopt-a-Burro program.

Gram Parsons (third from left), a musician and member of the Byrds and the Flying Burrito Brothers, strongly identified with the Joshua Tree area. He told friend Phil Kaufman that when he died he wanted to be cremated and his ashes strewn at Cap Rock. On September 19, 1973, Parsons died of an alcohol and narcotics overdose at the Joshua Tree Inn. Kaufman took Parsons's coffin from the Los Angeles airport and drove to Cap Rock, where he and a friend tried, with only partial success, to cremate Parsons's remains. The site is now famous with Parsons's fans. The group U2 further enhanced the monument's popular culture profile with the release of its 1987 album, *The Joshua Tree*. The album cover's lone Joshua tree was long assumed to be at Joshua Tree National Monument, and its location was a common question for Joshua Tree rangers. The iconic tree was actually located along Highway 190, west of Death Valley. (Above, courtesy of Barry Feinstein Photography; left, courtesy of U2360GRADI.)

Bob and Maureen Cates were active in the Sierra Club desert outing program, and they made many trips to Joshua Tree. Here, they stand atop the summit of Pinto Mountain in 1979. Bob wrote a popular guidebook for the monument, and he and Maureen formed their own company to publish it. They also organized a successful petition drive on behalf of the California Desert Protection Act and tried to get a peak at Joshua Tree named for Minerva Hoyt. (Courtesy of Bob and Maureen Cates.)

The Sierra Club's Elden Hughes was a tireless champion of the California desert. He became known for media-friendly sound bites that brought attention to the cause to pass California desert legislation. In 1985, Hughes met with resource chief Bob Moon, and they delineated areas for the proposed expansion of Joshua Tree. Nearly all of these lands, some 234,000 acres, made it into the final 1994 California Desert Protection Act, and many were designated as wilderness. (Courtesy of the Elden Hughes family.)

To commemorate passage of the California Desert Protection Act, a dedication ceremony was held at park headquarters on December 10, 1994. Amid speeches by legislators both in favor of and opposed to the legislation, a new sign over the entryway to the Oasis Visitor Center was unveiled, revealing the name Joshua Tree National Park. Dignitaries on hand for the ceremony included Secretary of the Interior Bruce Babbitt, Sen. Dianne Feinstein, and Congressmen Jerry Lewis and Bruce McCandless.

Sen. Dianne Feinstein has the honor of cutting a birthday cake for the new park as NPS maintenance foreman Gil Moreno watches. Moreno supervised the park's campgrounds and custodial programs. An excellent baker, he often made sheet cakes for special park events. Between 1999 and 2003, Senator Feinstein partnered with the Wildlands Conservancy to broker the purchase of 600,000 acres of former railroad lands from the Catellus Corporation, including 20,000 acres within Joshua Tree National Park.

Kaiser mined iron at Eagle Mountain from the mid-1940s until 1982. The proposal by Mine Reclamation Corporation, a Kaiser subsidiary, to use the inactive mine for a solid-waste landfill sparked an environmental battle that lasted more than 20 years. Environmentalists feared possible impacts to park air quality, wildlife, groundwater, and wilderness values. Once part of the original national monument, the Eagle Mountain iron deposits were excluded from the park by Congress in 1950. (Courtesy of Chris Clarke/KCET.)

A Twentynine Palms High School graduate, Ernest "Ernie" Quintana is a decorated veteran who pursued a career with the NPS. As superintendent of Joshua Tree from 1994 to 2002, Quintana strongly opposed the Eagle Mountain project, even after the NPS deputy director signed an agreement with the company to fund long-term monitoring of the landfill. His defense of Joshua Tree earned Quintana the National Parks Conservation Association's 1997 Stephen Tyng Mather Award. Quintana later became regional director of the NPS Midwest Region.

On Memorial Day weekend in 1999, a series of lightning strikes started wildfires that rapidly grew to 14,000 acres, forcing an emergency evacuation of park visitors. Between 1970 and 2000, desert fires were occurring with greater frequency and burning larger areas. Studies showed that the spread of exotic grasses created the fuel to carry fires across the Joshua tree woodland ecosystem. Park policy shifted to full suppression of wildfires in light of the uncertain ecological consequences.

Larry and Donna Charpied raise jojoba, a native desert shrub that produces a commercially valuable oil. Their 20-year battle over the Eagle Mountain Landfill ultimately reached the Supreme Court, where the court's refusal to hear an appeal from the Mine Reclamation Corporation effectively ended the landfill project. In 2005, the Charpieds received the Minerva Hoyt California Desert Conservation Award for their work opposing the landfill. They continue to battle industrial-scale projects adjacent to Joshua Tree National Park. (Courtesy of Jeff McLane.)

In 1966, the monument acquired Keys Ranch in a land exchange and faced a decision on how to manage the site. A debate ensued over whether the ranch should be carefully preserved or allowed to weather and decay naturally. When the ranch was added to the National Register of Historic Places, preservation won out. Rangers now conduct guided tours of the ranch for the public.

The Joshua Tree Natural History Association was created in 1962 to support science, education, and preservation programs at the park. In 1999, the park and the association started an adult education program, the Desert Institute, offering weekend field classes with recognized experts, guided hikes, and a community lecture series. Here, an institute class makes the return trip from the South Astrodome in the park's Wonderland of Rocks.

By the mid-1980s, mining in the monument had largely ceased as a viable activity. However, its effects posed significant problems for the NPS from a safety and liability standpoint. Open and unstable mine shafts were serious threats, and the amount of hazardous chemicals present at abandoned mines, including explosives, was largely unknown. The NPS evaluates mines for hazardous conditions and constructs gates or other barriers to keep out the unwary. Abandoned mines also have to be evaluated in terms of their historical value and their importance as wildlife habitat.

The Endangered Species Act changed how wildlife was managed at Joshua Tree and on all federal lands. The desert tortoise was declared a threatened species by the US Fish & Wildlife Service in 1990. Joshua Tree joined other desert land agencies in efforts to monitor tortoise populations, define threats to tortoises, and determine areas of critical habitat. Chris Collins, a wildlife technician at Joshua Tree, measures a tortoise in 2004 as part of a long-term data collection effort.

In 1969, the monument acquired a significant archeological collection that had belonged to Elizabeth Campbell. The Campbell Collection included artifacts dating from the early Pinto culture as well as pots, ollas, baskets, and other material from more recent native cultures. Storage was a major problem, as the monument lacked a professional museum facility. Archeological technician Stephanie Stephens inspects Campbell materials stored in a park garage bay around 1990.

In the 1970s and 1980s, a rapid increase in recreational climbing caught park managers unprepared. More than 4,000 climbing routes were identified by rangers with hundreds of routes and climbing bolts found in wilderness. Impacts to vegetation, growth of social trails, and damage to cultural sites by climbers became significant problems. After much controversy, a compromise with climbers was reached in 2000 that established a framework to manage climbing and monitor its impacts.

Joshua Tree has always been a park that has lived "off the grid." The developed area at Cottonwood, with its campground, visitor center, and housing area, used generator power and water from the spring itself. In the late 1990s, the park began to develop small solar arrays to power local sites within the park. A solar array at Cottonwood was built in 1998. At one time, Joshua Tree generated more solar power than all other national parks combined. (Courtesy of Robb Hannawacker.)

In the late 1990s, Joshua Tree received new authority to keep entrance and user fees it collected. Monies were to be used to improve visitor facilities and services. One early project was the construction of an amphitheater at Jumbo Rocks Campground. Rangers had long conducted evening programs for campers using gas-powered generators. The new building used solar power to operate projectors, lights, and sound system, greatly improving park ranger presentations.

To better serve visitors entering the park through the community of Joshua Tree, the Joshua Tree National Park Association acquired a private art gallery in December 2005 for use as a partner-owned NPS visitor center. The Joshua Tree Visitor Center opened in May 2006. On hand for the dedication are, from left to right, Nancy Downer (association executive director), Curt Sauer (superintendent), Tanie Boedekker (information specialist), Jon Stone (association president), and Joe Zarki (chief of interpretation).

The year 2011 marked the 75th anniversary of the Joshua Tree National Monument. Supt. Mark Butler and his staff created a yearlong program of activities to mark the historic occasion, and many new friends and partnerships were developed. In November, the park held its first employee reunion. More than 60 former Joshua Tree staff members turned up for the event, bringing several generations of park staff together to renew friendships and reflect on Joshua Tree's past and its future.

Historic Boundaries
Joshua Tree National Park and Monument
1936–1994

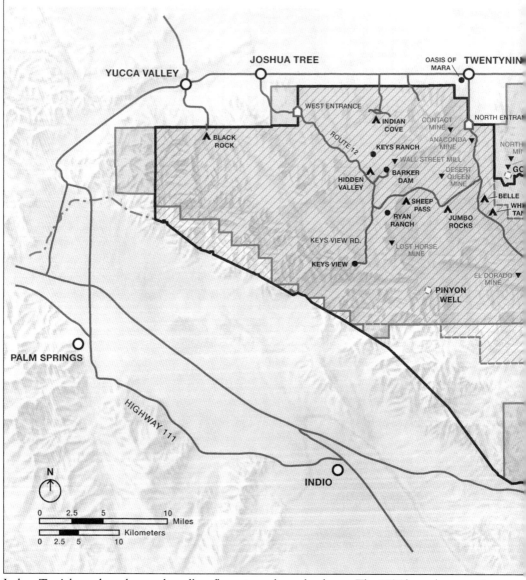

Joshua Tree's boundary changes broadly reflect views about the desert. The 1936 boundary remains its largest, showing Minerva Hoyt's determination to create a "grand park," incorporating the widest possible array of landforms, plants, and animals. The 1950 boundary set by Congress reflects pressure

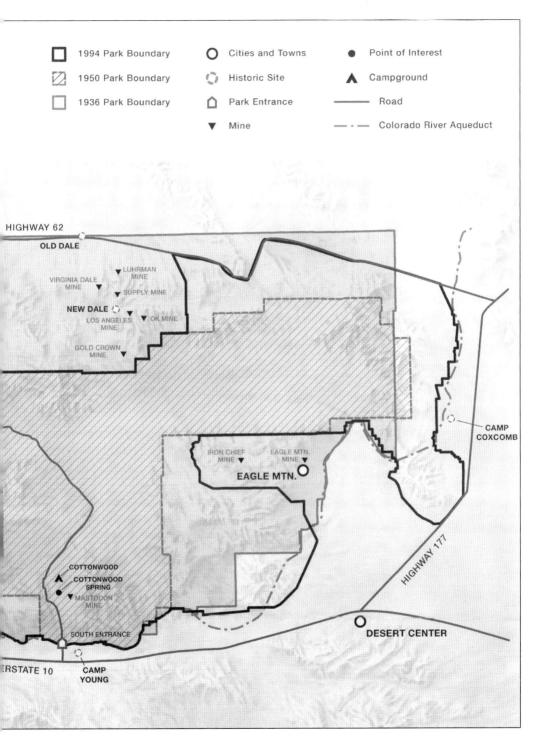

Legend:
- □ 1994 Park Boundary
- ▨ 1950 Park Boundary
- □ 1936 Park Boundary
- ○ Cities and Towns
- ◌ Historic Site
- ⌂ Park Entrance
- ▼ Mine
- ● Point of Interest
- ▲ Campground
- —— Road
- —·— Colorado River Aqueduct

HIGHWAY 62

OLD DALE

VIRGINIA DALE MINE ▼ · ▼ LUHRMAN MINE

▼ SUPPLY MINE

NEW DALE ◌

LOS ANGELES MINE ▼ · ▼ OK MINE

GOLD CROWN MINE ▼

CAMP COXCOMB

IRON CHIEF MINE ▼ · EAGLE MTN. MINE ▼

EAGLE MTN. ○

HIGHWAY 177

COTTONWOOD ▲

COTTONWOOD SPRING ●

▼ MASTODON MINE

SOUTH ENTRANCE

DESERT CENTER ○

INTERSTATE 10

CAMP YOUNG

from mining interests to exploit the area's minerals. The 1994 Desert Protection Act boundaries embody a maturing view of the desert and recognition of its unique qualities. (Map by Timothy Zarki using NPS map data.)

DISCOVER THOUSANDS OF LOCAL HISTORY BOOKS FEATURING MILLIONS OF VINTAGE IMAGES

Arcadia Publishing, the leading local history publisher in the United States, is committed to making history accessible and meaningful through publishing books that celebrate and preserve the heritage of America's people and places.

Find more books like this at
www.arcadiapublishing.com

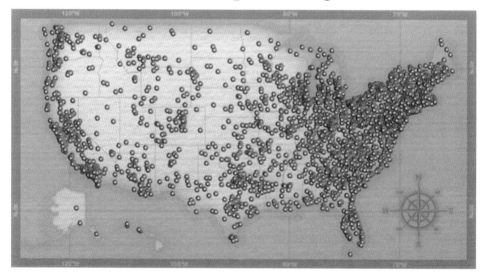

Search for your hometown history, your old stomping grounds, and even your favorite sports team.

Consistent with our mission to preserve history on a local level, this book was printed in South Carolina on American-made paper and manufactured entirely in the United States. Products carrying the accredited Forest Stewardship Council (FSC) label are printed on 100 percent FSC-certified paper.